Technology Planning

Technology Planning

Preparing and Updating a Library Technology Plan

Joseph R. Matthews

A Member of the Greenwood Publishing Group

Westport, Connecticut • London

Library of Congress Cataloging-in-Publication Data

Matthews, Joseph R.
  Technology planning : preparing and updating a library technology plan / Joseph R. Matthews.
    p. cm.
  Includes index.
  ISBN 1-59158-190-7 (pbk. : alk. paper)
  1. Libraries—Automation—Planning. 2. Libraries—Information technology—Planning. 3. Library planning. I. Title.
  Z678.9.M384 2004
  025'.00285—dc22   2004048774

British Library Cataloguing in Publication Data is available.

Copyright © 2004 by Joseph R. Matthews

All rights reserved. No portion of this book may be reproduced, by any process or technique, without the express written consent of the publisher.

Library of Congress Catalog Card Number: 2004048774
ISBN: 1–59158–190–7

First published in 2004

Libraries Unlimited, 88 Post Road West, Westport, CT 06881
A Member of the Greenwood Publishing Group, Inc.
www.lu.com

Printed in the United States of America

The paper used in this book complies with the Permanent Paper Standard issued by the National Information Standards Organization (Z39.48–1984).

10 9 8 7 6 5 4 3 2 1

Contents

Acknowledgments ix
Introduction xi

Chapter 1: Purpose and Need for a Technology Plan 1
   Why a Technology Plan? 3
   Purpose of the Plan 3
   Who Should Be Involved? 7
   Fundamental Issue 8
   Planning Resources 8
   Structure of a Technology Plan 9
   Suggested Web Resources 10
   Notes 12

Chapter 2: Description of the Library 13
   Mission Statement 15
   Sample Section from a Technology Plan 16
      1.0 Introduction 16
      1.1 History 16
      1.2 Description of the Library 16
      1.3 University and Library Mission Statements 17
      1.4 Staffing 19
      1.5 Budget/Expenditures 2001–2002 20
      1.6 Collection Size 20
      1.7 Collection Size Comparisons 21
      1.8 Library Automated Systems Technology Overview 22
   Notes 23

Chapter 3: Challenges Facing the Library 25
   SWOT Analysis 26
   Strategies 30
   Sample Section from a Technology Plan 33
      Section 2: Challenges Facing the Library 33
   Notes 38

Chapter 4: Emerging Technologies 41
    TCP/IP Everywhere 42
    Peer-to-Peer Networking..43
    XML...45
    Wireless Connections...46
    Voice and Translation Capabilities 47
    Web Services 48
        Custom Integration...48
        Middleware Product...48
        Web Services 48
    RFID 51
    Summary 51
    Notes 52

Chapter 5: Current Technology Environment...53
    Sample Section from a Technology Plan 57
        Current Technology Environment 57
    Notes 64

Chapter 6: Assessment of the Current Technology Environment............65
    Sample Section from a Technology Plan 73
        Assessment of Current Technology Environment 73
    Notes 82

Chapter 7: Evaluation of a Library's Web Site 83
    Web Site Design 84
        Usability Guidelines...88
    Evaluating Your Library's Web Site 90
    Sample Section from a Technology Plan 90
        Introduction..90
        Evaluation of SFPL's Web Site and Comparison to
            San Jose Library..91
        Recommendations..95
        Summary 96
    Notes 97

Chapter 8: Recommendations 99
    Sample Section from a Technology Plan 102
        Recommendations..102
        Summary 107
    Notes 109

Chapter 9: Updating the Plan 111
    How..113
    Who..114
    Summary 115
        Executive Summary 115
    Notes 118

Appendix A: Forms 119
    Form A. Current Technology Inventory 120
    Form B. Evaluation of Staff Skills..122
    Form C. Technology Assessment 124

Appendix B: Analysis of Library Information System Options 125
    Definitions..126
    Strengths and Weaknesses 127
        Control of Software...127
        Support Staff 128
        Infrastructure...129
        Implementation, Time Frames, and Conversion Cost........................130
        Implementation Cost Issues 131
        Transaction Volumes and Security Issues 132
    Cost Analysis 133
    Notes 134

    Index 135

Acknowledgments

This book has been improved considerably by a number of library school students who have taken a course on library information systems that I teach at the San Jose State University School of Library and Information Science. Most of these students have jobs at a wide variety of types of libraries and thus bring uniquely different perspectives to the course. They often ask wonderful questions that are insightful and stimulating.

These students are asked to prepare a technology plan for the library they work in or for a nearby library. I have selected the work of several students to include as examples in various chapters of this book. I particularly appreciate the willingness of these students to share their work. The students are Shawn P. Calhoun, Michael Hudson, Vivienne Khan, Dena Martin, Noreth Men, and John Wenzler.

I am also grateful for the timely and responsive interlibrary loan service provided by Teri Roudenbush and her staff at the California State University San Marcos library. Their energy is much appreciated! I also appreciate the efforts of Emma Bailey, Ron Mass, and Sharon DeJohn (whose copyediting skills are simply terrific) from Libraries Unlimited for making the publication of this book possible.

Joe Matthews
Carlsbad, California

Introduction

Planning for technology and the development of technology plans have generated considerable interest in the business, government, and library arenas, as evidenced by the numerous articles and conference presentations on this topic. The reason for this interest is readily apparent in that the planning looks ahead to determine what forms of hardware, software, and services will be required to meet the future needs of the library.

In the case of a public or school library, a library may prepare a technology plan, admittedly a brief plan, to qualify for an e-rate or LSTA grant from the state library. In other cases, a technology plan will help a library win a foundation grant. More often than not, the preparation of and/or updating of an existing technology plan will benefit an academic, a public, a school, or a special library because the library's funding decision makers and other interested stakeholders will see compelling evidence of the need for the planned changes so that the library's services can either stay constant or improve in the face of a constantly changing environment.

The preparation of a technology plan can have very positive benefits; it can

- ☐ Assist in aligning technology with other broader library and institutional objectives,
- ☐ Disseminate information to key decision makers and other stakeholders about technology needs and existing constraints,
- ☐ Assist in building alliances and creating bridges of communication so that others feel a sense of ownership concerning library issues,
- ☐ Help lobby for the necessary financial and other organizational resources needed to implement the technologies that will assist in providing needed services, and
- ☐ Assist in keeping an eye on the constantly changing technology itself.

Surprisingly, most of these benefits are social and economic rather than technical in nature.

As noted by Dwight D. Eisenhower, "plans are worthless, planning is everything."[1] *Planning* is a verb, and it implies action or a process. It is important for a library director and the library board to carefully consider who is involved in helping to prepare or update the library's technology plans. Each member asked to participate must be able to make a contribution to the plan. Contributions might entail understanding the potential impact of technology on a service or department, having an interest in keeping current with technology, and so forth. During this planning process, those involved in the planning process must question all present practices and assumptions about what the library is and the value it provides to its users.

One of the real benefits of the preparation of the technology plan is that staff will have a road map indicating the direction in which the library is proceeding. The plan connects the library's current and future technology with the goal of achieving the library's vision. The plan acknowledges that technology is a tool, admittedly a powerful and increasingly important tool, which will help the library achieve its service goals and objectives.

One of the pressing challenges associated with the use of technology is that there are continuous pressures to upgrade, change, revise, and add to what is already in place. And the reality of technology, especially the underlying infrastructure, is that a considerable amount of care and feeding is required. The skills of staff who are supporting the information technology within a library environment must be constantly improved and upgraded so that they can cope with an increasing variety of problems and threats to the security of the installed technologies.

The purpose of this book is to provide any library working to develop a technology plan with a general understanding of the components of a good technology plan. The book is intended to illustrate the concepts and issues involved with the preparation of a technology plan. It suggests a planning process that is suitable for all types and sizes of libraries and that can be used in the development of a stand-alone plan or a component of a larger organizational plan.

The field is not well seen from within the field.
—Ralph Waldo Emerson[2]

What Makes a Good Plan

A technology plan is good when it makes a difference. Most important, the plan helps the library make needed improvements in technology that support the library's ability to deliver quality library services. The plan might be responsible for the library's securing the required resources, since the funding decision makers gain a better understanding of the needs of the library and what role technology plays in helping the library achieve its objectives. A good plan is recognized by the following characteristics:

> ☐ *Concise:* The plan is as long as it needs to be and no longer. The plan explains what the needed improvements are and why they are needed. The plan is focused on using technology as a means to an

end—the end being providing library services that are of value to the library customers. A good plan will be well formatted and use tables and charts to more effectively communicate information. And it is important to remember that most people will not read the plan from cover to cover as if it were a novel but rather skip from section to section.

- ☐ *Specific:* The plan's recommendations are organized in a logical progression so that the dependencies of the recommendations are immediately apparent. As a document, the technology plan is readable (jargon is avoided or explained) and compelling. Typically the primary audience of a technology plan is the funding decision makers, who will most likely not be familiar with the operation of a library and, more than likely, will be a bit overwhelmed by technology itself.

- ☐ *Integrated:* The structure of the plan is such that there is a clear understanding of what is and what :eeds to be. All of the technology directly used by the library's customers and staff as well as the underlying infrastructure technologies are addressed by the plan. In this way all of the information about how technology is used to support the mission and vision of the library is presented in one coherent place.

- ☐ *Foreseeable:* Recognizing that technology is constantly changing and improving, the plan has a realistic time frame, that is, two to three years. A plan that has a longer planning horizon clearly is focusing on an anticipated environment that most likely will not exist (except in the planning document) given the chaotic and constantly changing nature of technology.

- ☐ *Flexible:* Obviously any plan must acknowledge that opportunities may arise or that some needs might change and thus the priorities within the plan should also change. The technology plan should be used not as a straitjacket but as a guide in helping the library move toward achieving its vision.

Conversely, a bad technology plan

- ☐ Will focus on technology for technology's sake.
- ☐ Does not explain how technology is used to support the mission of the library. There is not a clear explanation of how technology is being used to look after the needs of the library's customers.
- ☐ Does not explain why requested equipment, software, or services are needed.
- ☐ Is poorly organized and relies on using technobabble and jargon.

☐ Does not include all of the pertinent information (for example, a number of technology plans do not include the library's Web site address or assess the value and utility of the Web site).

Organization of the Book

This book is organized around the structure of a technology plan. A chapter is devoted to each section of the plan to more fully explain the subject areas to be covered in a specific section and how each section relates to other parts of the technology plan.

Chapter 1—Purpose and Need for a Technology Plan

The intent of this book is to provide information about a planning process that will, it is hoped, remove the techno mumble-jumble, so that the average layperson and library stakeholder can understand the need for technology in a specific library and how the specific recommendations in the library's technology plan have been determined. In short, the *what* and the *why* of the technology plan are explained.

Chapter 2—Description of the Library

The purpose of this chapter is to briefly describe the mission and goals of the library. What library services are offered and who is served are explained. Topics such as the library's budget, staffing, size of the collection, and a brief overview of what technology currently exists are presented.

Chapter 3—Challenges Facing the Library

Any library does not exist in a vacuum. Rather, a variety of forces are constantly at work as the environments within and outside the library are changing. This chapter suggests that the library prepare a SWOT (Strengths, Weaknesses, Opportunities, and Threats) analysis to better understand these forces. Once they are understood, the library can begin to plan in a way that both acknowledges, and takes advantage of, these forces.

Chapter 4—Emerging Technologies

Some technologies are more likely to have an impact, directly or indirectly, on a library and the services it provides. This chapter introduces and explains seven of these technologies that a library should be aware of. It suggests that the library staff should read not only the library literature but also some technology publications on a regular basis to stay better informed about these technologies.

Chapter 5—Current Technology Environment

A systematic description of the technology currently supporting the library is provided in this chapter. Topics addressed in this chapter include physical facilities, network infrastructure, servers, desktop computers, the automated library information system, software for desktops, technical support, and staff skills.

Chapter 6—Assessment of the Current Technology Environment

Given the technology currently being used by the library, it should be evaluated using a process that examines the risks of continuing to use the existing technology as well as the risks to the library of not implementing new technology.

Chapter 7—Evaluation of a Library's Web Site

The library's public face to those who do not visit the physical library is its Web site. Thus, the appearance, ease of use, and utility of information to be found on the Web site are very important. This chapter suggests ways for a library to evaluate its Web site and how to make improvements.

Chapter 8—Recommendations

This chapter pulls together the information about the changes to the existing technologies as well as the introduction of new technologies into a series of recommendations. These recommendations are then organized into a logical structure. A suggested budget and time frame for the changes is made along with identifying the benefits associated with making the changes. The benefits should be articulated so that the reader understands how the recommendations will benefit the library customer or staff member.

Chapter 9—Evaluation of the Plan

This chapter reviews the need for the library to periodically assess the continued relevance of its technology plan. Who should be involved and what topics should be addressed when the decision is made to update the plan are reviewed.

Appendix A—Forms

Several forms are provided that may be of value during the planning process.

Appendix B—Analysis of Library Information System Options

During the planning process the library may decide that it needs to replace its existing automated library information system with a new system. This appendix reviews the three broad choices that are available to and should be explored by the library: a stand-alone system, a shared system, and the use of system provided by an application service provider.

Notes

1. Dwight D. Eisenhower, speech to the National Defense Executive Reserve Conference, Washington, D.C., November 14, 1957.
2. Ralph Waldo Emerson. *Essays and English Traits, IX; Circles, 1841*. The Harvard Classics, 1909–1914. Available at www.bartleby.com/5/109.html (accessed August 1, 2004).

Chapter 1

Purpose and Need for a Technology Plan

> *Libraries cannot avoid planning. This is so, not only because of the complexity of their political and technological circumstances, and the constraints upon their resources, but also because formal planning is increasingly assumed and required in their organizational and professional environments.*—Ida Vincent[1]

The phrase *technology planning* has become so commonly used that its real meaning has become diluted or entirely lost. It is not the technology itself that should be the focus of the plan but rather the planning process, which is critical. The key is to focus on how the technology plan is merely the physical manifestation of a process that can become and remain a vital and important part of the life of any library.

Sometimes technology planning refers to the planning document itself. Much like a road map, the document can be used to demonstrate the direction in which one is traveling, the goal or objective of the trip, and the various paths to reach the desired destination.

Technology planning can also refer to the planning process. Depending upon the size of the library, a number of people may need to be involved in creating or updating a technology plan. It may also be necessary for the technology planning team members to obtain information from other organizational entities, for example, the information technology department, and various stakeholders. For some libraries, the responsibility for information technology infrastructure is placed in a separate department since it will serve the needs of a larger organization such as a university, city, or county. Stakeholders can provide information about the vision for the larger organization and plans and initiatives that are being put into place, and get a broader perspective about budgetary limitations, if any. The end result is that the group of people involved in creating or updating a technology plan has garnered the knowledge about what is needed to transform the concepts found within the planning document into an action plan that ensures the appropriate application of technology in the provision of quality library services.

Since the use of technology is simply a means to an end—that is, providing a service—then ultimately the plan itself is about people. If those involved are committed to working in a learning environment, then the creative genius of people can be released to accomplish common goals. Those involved in guiding the technology planning process must make sure that all participants are released from their regular duties to focus on the development of the technology plan.

Despite the importance of a technology plan, there are still a great many libraries, of all types, that do not have a technology plan. A survey conducted by the National Center for Technology Planning revealed that fewer than 30 percent of America's schools possess a written technology plan that is integrated into the curriculum,[2] or, if a technology plan has been prepared, it has been written to qualify for a grant.

A technology plan can be prepared in one of three ways:

1. *The larger (parent) organization has a technology plan that includes the library.* This approach ensures that the technology is more likely to be aligned with the goals and objectives of the total organization. One of the potential pitfalls of this approach from the library's perspective is that some of the unique needs of the library will not be recognized or not be afforded their proper place when needs are prioritized. In addition, time lines and goals may not be within the control of library managers.

2. *The library's technology plan is incorporated within the library's strategic or long-range plan.* The strength of this approach is that the library should be able to clearly link the needs of its customers and the services that the library provides with the plans being made for technology. The disadvantage with this approach is that the discussion and consideration of technology-based issues may involve individuals who should be spending their time on other important issues.

3. *The library has a separate technology plan.* The advantage of a separate technology plan for the library is that all issues arising from the potential use of technology can be carefully and systematically explored.[3] If the library is part of a larger organization, the needs of the library may not be reflected in a broader planning exercise.

In the view of the author, a separate technology plan for the library provides the greatest value for the library among the three options.

> **Tip!** The University of Michigan developed one of the best institutional technology plans. The plan was the result of a felt need for the university to re-examine its relationship to information and communication technologies given the rapidly changing nature of these environments. The report is entitled *President's Information Revolution Commission Report* (April 2001) and is available at: http://www.umich.edu/pres/inforev/.

Why a Technology Plan?

Technology, especially information technology, has become so integrated into the lives of most library staff members that the importance of sufficiently robust and reliable systems cannot be overstated. Staff members must be comfortable and knowledgeable in using technology to perform their everyday tasks and activities since jobs have become automation dependent.

Therefore, staff must be continually upgrading their skills and learning to use either new software products or new releases of existing systems. And in most cases, staff must forget some skills and knowledge that are no longer relevant or germane in the performance of their jobs.

Staff members are being called upon to respond to questions from their peers as well as assisting library customers when they encounter problems with technology. Thus, there is a need to develop and support a plan for maintaining existing technology as well as introducing new technology so that the library is able to deliver quality services that are valued by the library customer.

Purpose of the Plan

The library director must clearly identify the intended audience for the plan. In some cases, a plan is prepared in response to a requirement to secure funding. In this case, the plan must usually follow the guidelines of the agency disbursing the funds. However, the critical audience for a technology plan is the library stakeholders and funding decision makers who will determine the fiscal and other resources that are allocated to the library on a yearly basis. These decision-making individuals will, as a result of reading the plan, have a better understanding of how technology is used by the library to deliver services that are designed to meet the needs of its customers and will therefore be in a better position to allocate the necessary resources to fulfill the plan.

Everyone would agree that technology is to be found, to one degree or another, in almost all libraries today. Technology enables a library to evolve and offer new services, while at the same time technology in the broader environment pressures a library to change. Moreover, demanding customers will, in the end, give a library no choice but to change and embrace new technologies. The speed with which the Web is continuing to evolve and become a daily reality in providing the library's customers with access to all kinds of information is a reality that libraries must reckon with. Yet the question arises: Should the library be proactive or reactive in terms of technology planning?

According to March Osten:

> Strategic technology planning is a dynamic and reflective process that organizations engage in to seize the potential of advanced technologies. Strategic technology plans are grounded into your mission and fully integrated into your overall strategic plan. The strategic technology planning process ensures that you will clarify technological goals and establish priorities, organize relevant stakeholders and create evaluation systems—all before making hardware, software or Internet presence decisions.[4]

There are many reasons for preparing a technology plan. A technology plan can be used to

- Demonstrate to everyone—staff, customers, and other stakeholders—what the library is doing and planning on doing. In short, the library is cognizant of the need to manage technology just as it manages its other resources. And the plan can act as a training document to inform the stakeholders that the library has a clear and realistic plan for managing technology.

- Focus on the ways in which technology can assist the library in achieving its vision.

- Manage the budget process and expenditures to reduce the risks of acquiring unplanned (and unneeded?) equipment and software.

- Identify the strengths and weaknesses concerning the current implementation of technologies. In short, identify the gaps that exist.

- Prioritize the enhancements and new technology needed to assist the library in achieving its goals.

- Ensure that staff are aware of and trained in the use of new technologies and migrating to new versions of hardware and software.

- Demonstrate that the library is effectively using technology to deliver products and services to its customers.

- Create a fund-raising plan, if the financial resources are not available through the normal budgetary process, to implement the needed technology. The plan should drive the budget rather than the converse.

Even a casual observer would conclude that the purpose of technology planning is to look ahead and determine which forms of hardware, software, infrastructure, and technical support will be required to meet the future needs of the library. Yet a survey of those involved with technology planning suggested that the more common reasons for technology planning were

- Aligning technology with other institutional priorities,
- Building alliances with decision makers (inside and outside the library),
- Lobbying for (and obtaining) financial and other resources,
- Addressing existing technology needs, and
- Keeping an eye on the leading edge.[5]

These same individuals also suggested that the development of a technology plan fails to:

- Tie the use of technology to the institutional mission and priorities,
- Get the right people onboard,
- Limit the amount of technical detail, and
- Provide suitable leadership.

All agree that the importance of a good technology plan cannot be overstated. A technology plan can complement the collection development and staff development plans that most libraries create and maintain. And it plays a central part in any strategic plan of the library, increasingly so as technology consumes more and more of the library's budget.

A recent survey of financial executives found that organizations that align information technology (IT) strategies and plans with business strategies are significantly more likely to achieve a higher return on IT investment.[6]

> *Information technology is one of the four pillars of the library; the others are collections, staff and facilities.*
> —Robert E. Dugan[7]

As shown in Figure 1.1, the suggested planning process begins with a clear understanding of the library's mission and its vision for the future.

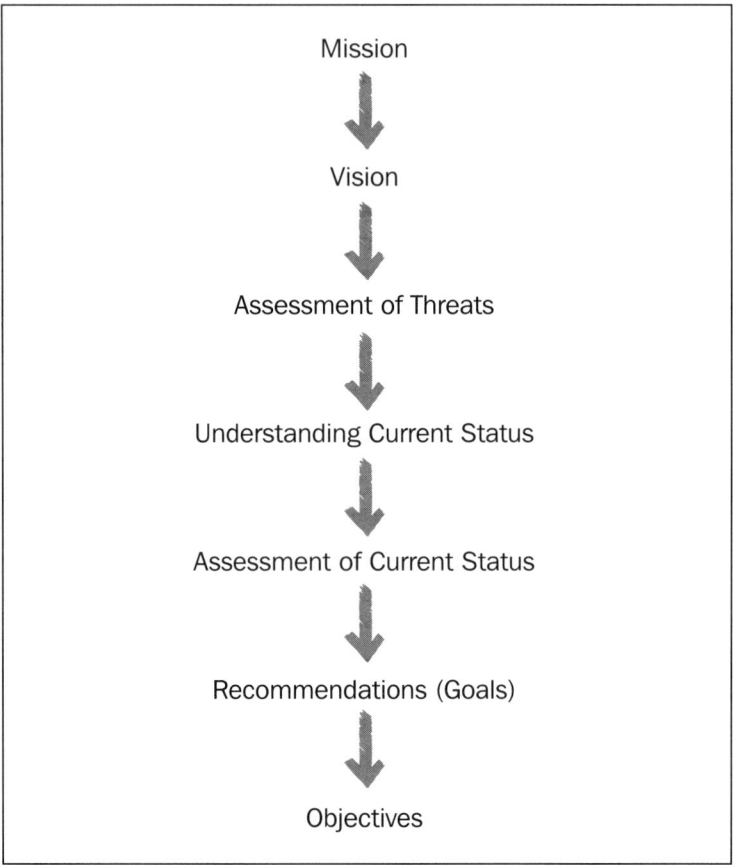

Figure 1.1. Planning Model

Objectives are specific and measurable targets for accomplishing goals. Objectives represent intermediate achievements necessary to realize goals. Good objectives will be SMART. That is, they will be

- **S**pecific. Objectives should generate specific actions and be detailed enough to be understandable and give clear directions to others.

- **M**easurable. A method for measuring an objective must be in place before work can begin. As such, a measure will determine when the objective has been accomplished.

- **A**ggressive but **A**ttainable. Objectives should be consistent with available resources but still cause library staff members to stretch to meet them.

- **R**esults-oriented. Rather than being general or vague, objectives should specify a result—an output or an outcome.
- **T**ime-bound. A specific deadline should be stated for achieving the objective. Generally the shorter the time frame for action, the better.

Who Should Be Involved?

Typically the library director will appoint a committee chairperson and assign committee members with the responsibility for preparing/updating the technology plan. The technology planning committee members should be drawn from the library's public services staff, technical services staff, and the technology support staff. In some cases, the library might want to recruit individuals from outside the library who are a part of the larger organization. Each member of the committee should be carefully chosen so that the individual's talents, expertise, and potential contributions are designed to complement those of the other committee members. In short, each committee member should have an active role to play rather than merely occupy a seat during meetings.

The size of the committee might range from two or three to a larger group, depending upon the size of the library. And the director should clearly establish a deadline for the completion of a draft of the plan. Again, depending upon the size of the library, the technology plan might be completed in a matter of a few weeks or stretch out over three to four months.

All other library staff members might be surveyed and asked what they think about their duties and responsibilities. Potential thought-provoking, leading questions to give staff include:

- I could finish this task faster if only . . .
- There must be an easier way to do this.
- I wish I had some technology device so I could . . .
- I wish I could be relieved on the monotony of this particular task.
- It would be nice to be able to do . . .
- I wish our local area network . . . (was faster, was more reliable, had more bandwidth)
- I wish our Internet connection was . . .
- I wish we had access to . . .
- I wonder what activities and services add real value for the library customer (and which of these should or should not be automated).

In a similar manner, the library's customers might be surveyed for a broad perspective, or focus groups could be used to gain more detailed understanding of the technologies that they would like to see the library provide or provide access to.

In addition, it is important to determine how various stakeholders (boards, city councils, board of supervisors, funding decision makers, administrators, the library's customers) should be involved. For example, should they only review a draft of the plan?

Fundamental Issue

The fundamental issue that must be addressed by any library as a part of its strategic planning process, and indirectly when the library is preparing a technology plan, is how to provide access to information. Planners should be able to answer the question: How accessible are information resources? Access should be provided in various forms:

- **Intellectual access:** Is the library providing a finding tool for information resources that are physically located only within the local library, or is it providing access to resources located at other libraries or at Internet Web sites?

- **Physical access:** The traditional way in which a library provides access to its information resources is by opening the library and allowing the library customer to use these resources without assistance, or by responding to customer requests for assistance.

- **Electronic access:** The library attempts to meet the institutional, research, and service needs of its customers by providing effective access to an array of electronic materials. Libraries will likely provide Internet access from within the library so that library users can access these resources. In addition, most libraries provide a service so that users can access the library's Web site and gain access to these electronic resources 24 hours a day, 7 days a week.

Planning Resources

Copies of the library's strategic or long-range plan, mission statement, vision statement, and existing or prior technology plans should be available for the committee members. In addition, it is helpful to provide a suggested table of contents of the proposed planning document so that the committee members know what the structure of the plan will be.

Structure of a Technology Plan

Just a cursory examination of a few technology plans prepared by libraries will reveal that there is no uniform format. However, in general terms, most technology plans will identify and evaluate the current situation, formulate a plan for improvement, and consider options for achieving the desired goals as identified in the plan. Effective technology plans, as judged by the fact that library staff and stakeholders are familiar with the planning document and routinely use it as a basis for taking action, can be relatively brief or fairly long. A good technology plan will be as long as it needs to be and no longer.

A suggested table of contents for a library technology plan is as follows:

1. **Executive Summary:** An executive summary provides a relatively short description—two to four pages—of the contents of the entire plan. The intent of the summary is to ensure that busy library stakeholders and administrators will understand the contents of the plan without having to read the entire thing. The executive summary is typically prepared once the entire plan has been completed.

2. **Description of the Library:** This section provides a brief description of the library and its mission statement. A description of the library's characteristics, including information about its budget, staff, and collection (size and type of materials), as well as information about how much the library is used (circulation, reference, etc.), is provided. The library's Web site address is noted.

3. **Challenges Facing the Library:** The library's vision statement is presented along with the current technology vision statement, if one exists (a library technology vision statement can be drafted, if needed). A SWOT (strengths, weaknesses, opportunities, and threats) analysis is prepared to identify issues that might affect future technology plans.

4. **Emerging Technologies:** Technologies that have the potential for affecting the services provided by a library and/or have a potential impact, either positive or negative, are identified and discussed in this section. For example, the use of audio and video streaming may require the library to provide additional bandwidth for its local area network.

5. **Current Technology Environment:** An inventory of equipment, software, network cabling, and staffing resources is prepared. This inventory includes information about the age, brand, capacity, version or release number, and other characteristics of the equipment and software operating in the library or on behalf of the library.

6. **Assessment of the Current Environment:** The current equipment and software are evaluated to determine whether any upgrades are needed or whether equipment and software should be added.

7. **Evaluation of the Library's Web Site:** An evaluation of the library's Web site's use, use of standard software and Internet protocols, as well as usability (may want to compare to other similar Web sites), is prepared.

8. **A Plan for Action:** Possible enhancements and changes to the existing technology found within the library are identified. Related items are grouped together and a preliminary plan for action is developed.

9. **Recommendations:** A list of proposed enhancements, upgrades, replacements, and new components is presented together with a budget, an estimate of the likely benefits, and a suggested implementation time line. The recommendations should be realistic given the library's available resources.

10. **Updating the Plan:** The value and utility of the plan should be assessed periodically, given the speed with which technology continues to change and the needs of the library's customers are evolving. Thus, periodic meetings should be scheduled to ensure that the plan is being implemented on schedule. The decision about when to prepare an update should also be considered on an annual basis.

Appendixes might be included so that information that is relevant to the plan is immediately available for the interested reader but is not included within the body of the plan, as most readers would need to review this material. Such appendixes might contain network diagrams, a detailed inventory of hardware and software, and other pertinent information.

Each of the suggested sections for a library technology plan is discussed in greater detail in the following chapters of this book. But one fundamental caveat for any plan is that it must be flexible and generic enough to allow for unknown events and for the library to adjust to them.

Suggested Web Resources

Helping.Org provides a number of resources related to technology and technology planning: http://www.helping.org/nonprofit/howyouwork.adp#techplanning.

Internet Surveys provides access to a variety of Net-based surveys of potential interest to libraries: http://www.clickz.com/stats/.

Library Research Planning, a Web site hosted by the Colorado State Library and the University of Denver, provides access to a wide variety of technology, demographic, and library statistics: http://www.lrs.org.

Library Technology Planning, provided by the Wisconsin Department of Public Instruction, Public Library Development. has a valuable set of resources: http://www.dpi.state.wi.us/dlcl/pld/planout.html.

The **LINC Project** has compiled a collection of tips and thinking-points to get a group started on a technology planning and assessment process: http://www.lincproject.org/toolkit/tech_strategies.htm.

National Center for Technology Planning provides a set of resources designed primarily for schools and higher education institutions: http://www.nctp.com/.

North Central Regional Educational Laboratory is a nonprofit organization designed to help schools achieve their full potential: http://www.ncrel.org/tandl/homepg.htm.

Npower has developed a number of resources that relate to technology planning and assessments. Included is a tool for assessing an organization's tech-savvy as well as its existing technology needs. Users rate their organization's technology practices against "best practices" benchmarks by responding to a series of questions. One section deals specifically with best practices benchmarks for technology planning, so users can quickly see how they compare: http://www.npowerseattle.org/tools/index.htm.

The Special Library Association provides a set of resources and links to other technology planning information sources: http://www.sla.org.

TechAtlas is an online "do-it-yourself" technology assessment and planning tool. An online questionnaire asks about the organization and its technology systems, then makes recommendations that can help guide the organization's technology planning for the future: http://www.techatlas.org/tools/.

Tech Soup is the technology place for nonprofits. A large number of articles and other resources are available pertaining to technology and technology planning: http://www.techsoup.org/howto/index.cfm.

Technology Trends for Libraries, provided by the Library and Information Technology Association of ALA, can be found by doing a search for "Technology Trends" from the ALA home page: http://www.ala.org.

The Texas Center for Educational Technology provides links to Web resources designed for schools: http://www.tcet.unt.edu/tek-plan.htm.

Notes

1. Ida Vincent. Strategic Planning and Libraries: Does the Model Fit? *Journal of Library Administration*, 9 (3), 1988, 45

2. Larry S. Anderson. *Technology Planning: Receipt for Success.* March 1994. Available at: www.nctp.com/tp.recipe.html (accessed August 1, 2004).

3. Robert E. Dugan. Information Technology Plans. *The Journal of Academic Librarianship*, 28 (3), May 2002, 152–56.

4. March Osten. *Strategic Technology Planning: What Is It?* January 4, 2001. Available at: http://techsoup.org/articlepage.cfm?Articleid=267&topicid=11 (accessed August 1, 2004).

5. Martin Ringle and Danile Updegrove. Is Strategic Planning for Technology an Oxymoron? *CAUSE/EFFECT*, 21 (1), 1998, 18–23.

6. Allen Bernard. *Majority of IT and Business Plans Still Not Linked.* March 5, 2004. Available at: www.clickz.com/stats/markets/professional/article.php/3305971 (accessed August 1, 2004).

7. Robert E. Dugan. Information Technology Plans, 152.

Chapter 2
Description of the Library

> *One machine can do the work of fifty ordinary men. No machine can do the work of one extraordinary man.*—Elbert Hubbard[1]

The first section of the library's technology plan should convey to the reader a compelling, comprehensive, and comprehensible description of the library and its services. A brief description of the library and its mission statement should be included. A description of the library's characteristics, including information about its budget, staff, and collection (size and type of materials), as well as information about how much the library is used (circulation, reference, etc.), should be part of this section also. Include the library's Web site address. Remember that the audience for the plan is primarily those policy makers and funding decision makers who are not familiar with the operation of your library and its associated jargon. If you use any acronyms, for example LSTA, they must be spelled out and then abbreviated: Library Services and Technology Act (LSTA). You can't assume that the reader will know your library's acronyms or jargon.

Section headings for a technology plan should be used and might include the following:

- Introduction (to the plan and how it is organized).

- Purpose of This Plan. The reason a technology plan was prepared for the library should be explained.

- History. A brief review of the library's history should be presented so that the reader has some appreciation of the origins and evolution of the library.

- Physical Description. Include, for example, the date the building was constructed, the date the building was remodeled, square feet, number of chairs (seats), and hours open each week.
- Mission Statement.
- Community Served. Include the total size of the population served, the proportion of the population that has registered and received a library card, and a description of the demographic characteristics of the population. It may be of interest to identify the proportion of registered borrowers who are active library customers.
- Staffing. List the total number of librarians, paraprofessionals, and clerical staff (usually expressed as full-time equivalents or FTE) and their typical duties. It would be helpful to know what portion of the staff is in technical services and in public services (not applicable for small libraries).
- Budget. State the total library budget and some summary categories (rather than a listing of all line items). Useful categories include salaries (with fringe benefits), materials or acquisitions (books, A/V, magazines, online databases, other materials), technology (computer hardware, software, maintenance services, leased lines, etc.), and operations (utilities, maintenance, supplies, etc.). It is helpful to compare the current year's budget with that of the budgets from prior years to assist the reader in identifying any trends. The budgets from comparable libraries may also be of value.
- Collection Size and Annual Growth. Describe the type of materials to be found in the library, number of titles and volumes added each year, volumes withdrawn, and so forth.
- Services Offered. Describe the range of services provided by the library that are designed to meet the needs of the library's potential customer base.
- Use of the Library. Include the amount of in-library use, materials checked out by library patrons, use of reference services, attendance at programs, and so forth. Providing information about the use of other "comparable" libraries may be useful so that the reader has a better sense of how the local library is doing.
- Technology. Provide the name of automated system installed in the library and the number of computer workstations available for public use and staff use.

Tables, photos, and charts, as needed, are also helpful to improve the "readability" of this document for the reader, for example, a table or chart of the budget categories. Always consider whether information that might be of interest to some but not all readers might be more appropriately placed in an appendix.

If you have multiple libraries, a map might be helpful to show the relative location of each facility. A table to indicate summary information about all of the libraries might also be useful.

Mission Statement

A mission statement is a brief, comprehensive statement that identifies why and for whom a library exists. The mission statement describes customers and the products and services offered to them that will be of value. Since some libraries have not created a mission statement, it might be wise to do so or to consider revising the existing statement.

A good mission statement will

- Identify the overall purpose of the library in broad terms,
- Identify the basic needs the library is attempting to fill,
- Recognize the customers of the library, and
- Identify the products and services provided.

A memorable mission statement will be relatively brief (one to two sentences at most) and will avoid the use of library jargon.

The value of stating the mission statement in the technology plan is that it helps the reader understand the basic objectives that the library is attempting to fulfill and ensures that the following elements of the plan reflect the library's or parent organization's mission. There is nothing worse, in terms of frustration and money potentially misspent, than the technology in a library moving in one direction while the library (and possibly the larger organization) is moving in another.

With a clear understanding of the library's mission and whom it is attempting to serve, the library will establish service goals for its customers. It is these service goals that help the library to organize its products and services to meet the needs of its customers. For public libraries, the service goals are typically referred to as service objectives.[2] Special libraries typically have a clear focus on helping their customers achieve clear productivity improvement or cost reduction objectives.

Technology should be viewed as a vehicle to offer more efficient and effective delivery of current services and to offer new services to assist the library in achieving its mission.

16 \ 2—Description of the Library

The following sample section illustrates how the reader can be provided with a quick overview of the library. It must be remembered that the primary audience for a technology plan is the various stakeholders who control the financial and other resources that are made available to the library. These individuals are typically not very "library literate," and thus the use of library jargon must be avoided (or must be explained in layperson's terms if used).

Sample Section from a Technology Plan[3]

1.0 Introduction

This technology plan is for the Private University learning center and offers an assessment of the current state of technology. It includes ideas and input for directions the library may consider in the future as the technology landscape changes both on campus as well as outside the university.

1.1 History

The Library building is more than 30 years old and provides its patrons with access to its collection and reference and circulation services.

1.2 Description of the Library

The Library has approximately 100,000 square feet of combined use space. As of spring 2001 there were 708 seats in the library, and at this time there are no plans to add seats or expand library square footage.

1.2.1 Community Access to Library Technology

The use of library resources is generally limited to students, faculty, staff, and others with ties to the communities served by the Private University. While the general public has limited access to the online catalog or OPAC, all other resources (databases, indexes, physical resources such as personal computers, etc.) have limited access.

Campus community members have access to the following technology resources:

    Reference services/labs

        - 30 Windows PCs
        - 5 Macintosh computers
        - 5 networked printers

Electronic classroom
- 25 personal computers and advanced classroom technologies

ITS (Information Technologies Services, a separate department)
- first-floor lab—15 personal computers, one network printer
- second-floor lab—25 personal computers, 2 networked printers

Wireless and wired building
- Unlimited wireless (802.11b) access in first-floor atrium (50 seats)
- Over 50 hot-Ethernet ports on first to fourth floors of library

Users purchase their own personal digital assistant (PDA) or laptop wire/wireless modem from a list of devices supported by the information technology services (ITS) department.

Remote
- Dial-in access with over 400 modems
- Unlimited OPAC access
- All databases are password protected by ITS-generated individual password/access ID.

1.3 University and Library Mission Statements

The library operates as a division of academic affairs within the university under the direction of the campus provost. As such, the library's mission is derived from, and attempts to directly reflect, the mission and values of Private University.

1.3.1 Mission and Values

The university's current mission and values statements follow.

The University's core values include a belief in and a commitment to advancing:

- The freedom and the responsibility to pursue truth and follow evidence to its conclusion;
- Learning as a humanizing, social activity rather than a competitive exercise;
- A common good that transcends the interests of particular individuals or groups, and reasoned discourse rather than coercion as the norm for decision making;

- Diversity of perspectives, experiences, and traditions as essential components of a quality education in our global context;
- Excellence as the standard for teaching, scholarship, creative expression, and service to the university community;
- Social responsibility in fulfilling the university's mission to create, communicate, and apply knowledge to a world shared by all people and held in trust for future generations;
- The moral dimension of every significant human choice: taking seriously how and who we choose to be in the world;
- The full, integral development of each person and all persons, with the belief that no individual or group may rightfully prosper at the expense of others; and
- A culture of service that respects and promotes the dignity of every person.

The following initiatives are key to the university's achieving recognition as a premier university:

1. Recruit and retain a diverse faculty of outstanding teachers and scholars and a diverse, highly qualified, service-oriented staff committed to advancing the university's mission and its core values.
2. Enroll, support, and graduate a diverse student body, which demonstrates high academic achievement, strong leadership capability, concern for others, and a sense of responsibility for the weak and the vulnerable.
3. Provide an attractive campus environment and the resources necessary to promote learning throughout the university:
    - Technology solutions to enhance learning and improve service,
    - Facilities to support outstanding educational programs, and
    - Learning resources that improve the curriculum and support scholarship.

1.3.2 Library Mission Statement

The library primarily provides support to academic programs by making available the broadest possible array of learning and information resources for instruction and research support.

Its role is further defined by the expression of specific objectives:

1. To make available the books, periodicals, governmental publications, audiovisual, and other library materials necessary for conducting a successful library program.

2. To build a competent library staff to service and interpret collections.

3. To provide the physical facilities and equipment that will assist in the use of the collections.

4. To assist and cooperate with faculty members in their varied instructional and research programs.

5. To encourage students to develop the habit of self-education and lifelong learning skills.

6. To offer a program of library service that will not only meet but also exceed the requirements and standards of the various professional associations and accrediting agencies.

7. To integrate the library program with local, regional, national, and international libraries to create "a virtual library."

8. To provide select services to special noninstructional constituencies.

1.4 Staffing

As of May 2001:

Professional Staff (MLIS Librarians)	17
Support Staff/Professionals	22
Student Assistants (FTE)	18
Total FTE	57

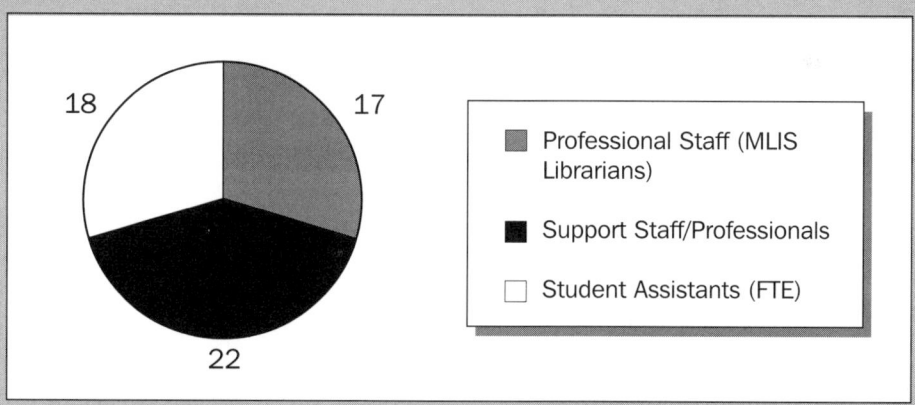

Figure 2.1. Staffing Levels

The largest numbers of librarians are in the Reference and Distance Services division (12) and the smallest number (1) is in Systems. Technical Services (acquisitions and cataloging) has two librarians, Circulation has one, and each regional library has one MLIS librarian.

2—Description of the Library

Currently one support staff member is enrolled in an MLIS program, and there are two MLIS interns working in the reference department (unpaid and not included in the statistics above).

1.4.1 Library Organization

The organization is relatively flat, with few managers reporting to other managers, who in turn report to the dean.

1.5 Budget/Expenditures 2001–2002

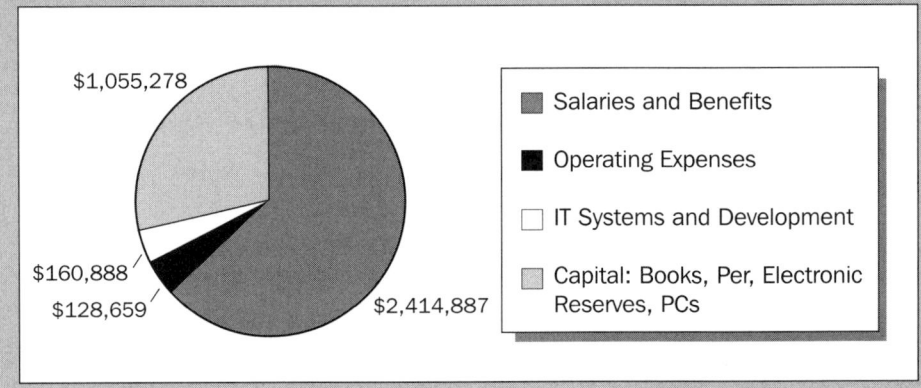

Figure 2.2. Components of the Budget

There are no telecommunications charge-backs to the library. In the current campus charge-back process, the library does not pay for on- or off-campus connectivity.

1.6 Collection Size

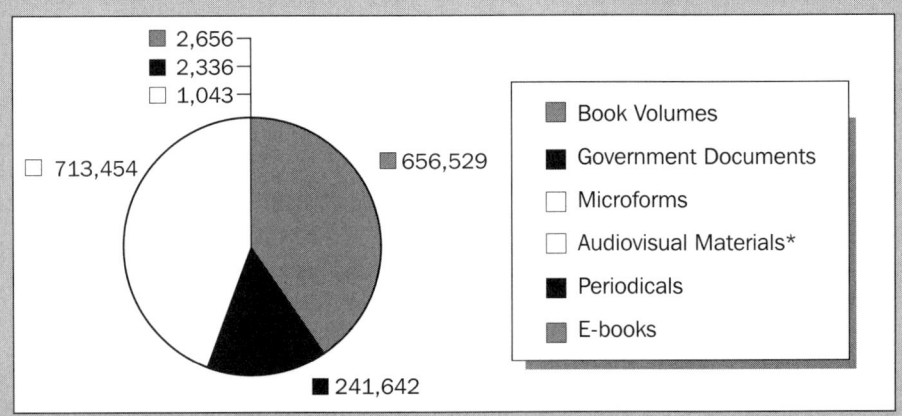

Figure 2.3. 2001–2002 Summary Statistics
*AV materials recently transferred to library from separate campus department.

1.7 Collection Size Comparisons

Using the most recent Association of College and Research Libraries (ACRL) statistics published in 2000, Private University compares favorably to other doctorate-granting institutions.

1.7.1 ILL/Document Delivery

An interlibrary loan service allows patrons to request titles/select books either not carried or currently checked out. Turn around (time to pick-up) is generally 2 business days, and items can be checked out for approximately 14 calendar days.

Borrowing	2000–2001	2001–2002
Books and dissertations	855	381
Link Plus	800	2,644
Photocopies	1,576	1,017
Total borrowing	3,231	4,042
Lending	**2000–2001**	**2001–2002**
Books and dissertations	1,965	1,512
Link Plus	1,022	2,436
Photocopies	259	526
Total lending	3,246	4,474

Clearly the ILL service has had a significant impact on the library, and extends the catalog to in effect add access to the more than 35 member libraries in the state. While there are processing issues and resources required, the technical impacts are minimal.

1.7.2 Document Delivery

Document delivery represents the requests the library receives from patrons to copy and deliver unique documents (generally items that do not circulate such as current periodicals and rare books/special collection items).

Document Delivery	2000–2001	2001–2002
Total requests filled	3,073	4,203

1.7.3 Circulation and Reserve Statistics

Circulation statistics are all items checked out by all patron types. They do not include reference items or noncirculating items such as reserve materials.

Circulation Statistics	2000–2001	2001–2002	% Change
All patrons	67,220	69,549	3.46

1.7.4 Reserve Statistics

Reserve items are generally noncirculating items such as course readers maintained by faculty for library use only by students.

Reserve Statistics	2000–2001	2001–2002	% Change
All patrons	12,067	14,622	21.17

1.7.5 Library Gate Counts

The library counts patrons as they exit the library. No determination is made about length of stay, purpose, or correlations to circulation, reserves etc.

Exit Turnstile Counts	2000–2001	2001–2002	% Change
	350,925	347,802	-0.9

The decline in gate count is under analysis.

1.8 Library Automated Systems Technology Overview

Private University has been running Innovated Interfaces Inc. (III) since its original retrospective conversion in the mid-1990s. The university runs all Millennium versions of the following III modules (and submodules):

- Cataloging
- Circulation and Reserves
- Web OPAC
- Materials Booking
- Management Reporting

Every library staff member has integrated access to all necessary systems at his or her desktop. The library benefits from the campus use of two T1 lines supporting over 3 Mbps of bandwidth.

1.8.1 OPAC Requirements

The library OPACs are fully accessible from any computer running a standard Web browser. Private University's ITS department establishes browser support guidelines and is responsible for all browsers on publicly accessible PCs (owned by the library or ITS). In addition, the ITS department establishes baseline PC (and Mac) requirements and purchases, installs, and supports all publicly accessible machines in the library. The library does not run any software on any publicly accessible PC, nor is the library responsible for security or network access passwords. It is understood from the ITS technology plan that this will be the trend going forward, and accordingly the library has not budgeted resources to alter the course.

1.8.2 Future Challenges—LibQual + Findings

During the 2002 school year the library conducted a survey of students called LibQual+, faculty and staff with the explicit goal of assessing their overall satisfaction with the library and its services. The Association of Research Libraries (ARL), under the auspices and guidance of both ARL and ACRL (Association of College and Research Libraries), designed the survey. The research response was very high (over 10 percent of the campus population of nearly 10,000), and the needs were clear: Online, full-text journals are the predominant item our constituents need.

1.8.3 Campus Technology

There are two primary projects underway on campus in the ITS domain that will affect the library's ability to deliver services needing bandwidth. Currently, all buildings on campus are having their data closets, and all internal switching equipment, upgraded and standardized to a suite of preferred vendors (Cisco and Sun), and a campuswide structured cabling program is being run in support.

Second, the university has founded a technology assessment and improvement task force chaired by a member of the university's board of trustees. In addition to standards, the threads necessary to tie technology to the department level (e.g., the library), the learning communities (e.g., academic affairs), and the annual budgeting processes are now institutionalized and transparent to all who rely on these services.

Notes

1. From *Bartlett's Familiar Quotations,* 16th ed., Justin Kaplan, general editor (Boston: Little, Brown, 1992).

2. Ethel Himmel and William James Wilson. *Planning for Results: A Public Library Transformation Process.* Chicago, American Library Association, 1998.

3. This section of a technology plan was prepared by Shawn P. Calhoun.

Challenges Facing the Library

> *Change is not made without inconvenience, even from worse to better.*—Richard Hooker[1]

Once the reader has become familiar with the mission and roles of the library, its budget, the services it provides, and how much those services are utilized, the next section of the technology plan focuses on the challenges facing the library. The destination, or where the library would like to be in the next three to four years, is often called a vision statement. The technology plan must have an adequate vision statement as its starting point.

The vision statement sets out long-term targets and success criteria for the library and acts as a focus for identifying the key strategic activities that must be accomplished if the vision is to be achieved.[2] A good vision statement is clear, brief, memorable, motivating, and customer-related. If a vision statement is too long, then it will fail the test of being memorable. And unless the vision is focused on meeting customer needs, then the reason for the library is being ignored.

Quite clearly the goal for any library is to remain in "synch" with its customers so that it can better serve their needs. Often sharing a draft of the vision statement with the library's stakeholders will elicit comments and remarks that will allow the library to quickly determine whether its vision is "in tune" or "resonates" with these important constituents.

A vision that will inspire and challenge provides more than a picture of the library's ideal future. The vision

- Represents a continual purpose of the library,
- Invigorates and challenges,
- Is a critical ingredient for change,
- Will have a positive effect on the values and behaviors of staff members, and
- Is the definitive standard against which all progress is measured.

Leadership is the ability to transform vision into reality. To be successful, top library managers must consistently convey the organization's mission, strategic direction, and vision to employees, customers, and funding decision makers. A clear, concise statement that communicates what the organization is and is not and where the library intends to go increases the likelihood that employee actions will be aligned with the library's vision.

Having a clearly articulated and written vision provides a perspective on being aware of where you are (and where you have come from) and knowing where you are heading. Since there are many possible destinations, knowing the desired target allows the library and its staff members to make better decisions and choices as the future unfolds. Having a specific destination allows the library to focus rather than attempting to be all things to all people (and, of necessity, doing most of these things poorly).

The team developing the technology plan can use the library's vision statement as a basis for developing a technology vision statement that articulates the supporting role of technology in delivering services to the library's customers. Such an approach should provide clarity in the decision-making process and a more focused way to allocate resources.

SWOT Analysis

Assessing the environment within which the library exists is an important first step in any planning process. Assessing the context of the current and likely future environment helps to determine what factors will affect the library. What trends, government regulations, and technology changes will likely affect the organization? Who are the library's competitors, and how well is your library doing in the competitive environment?

In determining the direction and possible strategies of the future of any institution, it helps to take stock of current situations, outlooks, and prospects. One of the most popular planning tools to assist in accomplishing this is a "SWOT" analysis, or an examination of the library's **S**trengths, **W**eaknesses, **O**pportunities, and **T**hreats, as shown in Figure 3.1. An alternative acronym,

WOTS UP (Weaknesses, Opportunities, Threats, and Strengths Underlying Planning), is sometimes used.

	Internal (Within the library)	External (Outside the library)
Positive	Strengths	Opportunities
Negative	Weaknesses	Threats

Figure 3.1 SWOT Analysis

Typically the SWOT analysis starts with an inward-looking or internal focus. One of the challenges of such an analysis is achieving a balanced and objective perspective. At times it is difficult to identify the strengths or acknowledge the limitations of the library. The quality of the library's collection, staff, infrastructure, organizational structure, location and condition of facilities, services, programs, and funding, for example, may be either a strength or a weakness. Some libraries have used surveys and focus groups in an attempt to better understand the library and its services from the perspective of the customer. Such surveys are particularly appropriate in the planning process and would be undertaken as a preliminary step.

Once the internal assessment has been completed, attention shifts to an external focus. Here too it may be difficult to objectively assess what is happening in the external environment without checking a variety of information resources. One helpful technique is to remember to use the mnemonic "TEMPLES" when considering the external arena.[3] "TEMPLES" stands for

- **Technology:** What are the important technologies and technology-based standards that might have an impact on the library and its ability to provide new or enhanced services? Important technology trends that a library should be aware of and carefully consider are reviewed in greater detail in the next chapter. One of the challenges in this area is to not overestimate the rate at which library users will adopt technology.[4] What are the potential effects of the World Wide Web on providing library services? Should wireless play a more important role in the library? How long will it be before your current equipment and software become obsolete?

- **Economy:** What is happening with the economy, and would a downturn or expansion in the state or local economy have an impact on the library's budget? Will a downturn in the economy have an impact on demand for services? Do inflation or the exchange rate affect your library? Do the rising levels of consumer spending affect your library?

- **Markets:** Would the ever-changing marketplace (for information resources and services provided by a library) create a new competitor or provide a new opportunity for the library? For example, are Internet-based reference services (Ask-a-Question) a competitor and/or a resource? Is the fact that millions of people turn first to Internet search engines such as Google before they even consider a library troubling? Does your library understand who its primary customers are and the value they receive from using the library? Do you know who your competitors are (and their strengths and weaknesses)? Has your library explored introducing new services and discontinuing others?

- **Politics:** Is there a change in the political environment that might have an impact on local, state, or national governments? Is government likely to introduce regulations that will affect your library?

- **Law:** Are there any federal, state, or local laws that might have an impact on the local library? Changes in administrative law and regulations might also require a change in service offerings at your library. Are there any potential impacts from current and outstanding court cases. Will changes in environmental regulations, health and safety rules, and employment law affect the library?

- **Ethics:** Are there clear policies regarding how the library acquires materials and services? For example, are library policies concerning copyright in compliance with the law and followed by all staff members?

- **Society:** Is society changing in ways that require a reexamination of the mission, goals, and vision of the library? Are the demographic characteristics of the library's customers changing? Do your customers expect to be involved in the planning of library services? Will expectations regarding quality of life, leisure time, and vacations affect your library?

Some of the issues that might affect a library are shown in Table 3.1.

Table 3.1. Opportunities and Threats Facing a Library

	Opportunities	Threats
Technology	• Videoconferencing • Distance learning • Increase networking with other agencies. • Consider use of RFID. • Amount of information available online is proliferating. • Ability to access, evaluate, and synthesize information is important.	• Staff's lack of technical knowledge • Staff who are reluctant to embrace new technologies • Information technology is rapidly emerging and changing. • Information is accessible quickly without an intermediary.
Economy	• Recovery program for materials not returned. • Improve facilities.	• Budget and lack of funding • Lack of skilled staff • Increasing costs limit access to electronic information.
Markets	• Marketing collections and services • Publicize particular databases since particular groups of customers could benefit from knowing where to find information. • Build partnerships with other institutions/agencies. • More interesting marketing would create awareness that services exist. • Increase collections in specific target areas.	• Competing businesses such as mega-bookstores • Commercial online search and reference Web sites • Fee-based reference services from the Internet
Politics	• Continue to build a strong relationship with the various funding decision makers.	• Dysfunctional organizational systems • Public policy vs. library policy • Stakeholders looking for increased accountability

Table 3.1. (*Cont.*)

	Opportunities	Threats
Law	• Ensure that library policies comply with various laws.	• Library policies may conflict with newly enacted laws, for example, the Patriot Act.
Ethics	• Better accountability of meaningful goals and measures • Create a connection with people who do not see the library as part of their lives.	• Outside influences from government agencies
Society	• Classes in new technologies • Ongoing staff training • Staff/patrons embrace change.	• Patron/staff resistance to change

Once the issues in each of these areas have been identified and assessed, then the library can determine the impact these issues have on meeting the service goals of the library. And more specifically, it can determine the extent to which technology can assist in overcoming some of the issues it faces.

Strategies

A strategy is a plan of action with a shared understanding designed to accomplish a specific goal that focuses on how a given set of objectives will be achieved. Strategies are designed to eliminate the gap that exists between where the library is today and where it wants to be tomorrow. Strategies are *not* the programmatic goals and objectives that most libraries have historically developed on an annual basis. For example, some libraries develop programmatic goals that can be grouped into several categories (services, technology, resources, staff development). Such an approach does not reflect a coherent set of strategies but is rather a potpourri of goals and objectives and represents a strategy known as "more of the same."

Strategies are about making choices and, when required, deliberately choosing to be different. As such, a strategy allows an organization to create a sustainable advantage. Strategy recognizes that it is not possible to be all things to all people and thus focuses on choices.

Books and articles about strategy will sometimes mention the acronym MOST (mission, objectives, strategy, tactics), which suggests that there is a structure and order to strategy development. Using the organization's mission statement as the starting point, objectives are defined, strategies developed, and short-term tactics agreed upon. Regrettably the process of developing winning strategies is much more disordered, iterative, and normally determined through a trial-and-error process.[5]

Ultimately, a strategy should be judged by how well it delivers long-term added value for the customers of the organization. How a library adds value is reflective of its core competencies and how well it delivers its services to meet the needs of its customers. Identifying the ways in which the library adds value and what are the appropriate strategies for a library to pursue is the responsibility of the management team for the library. In short, focusing on the "big picture" is much more important than the operational day-to-day crises that seem to occupy so much time of library staff members, a proclivity they share with most organizations.

There are three broad strategies that can be considered should a library wish to increase its responsiveness to its community of customers: customer intimacy, innovative services, and operational excellence.[6] These three broad interconnected strategies are shown in Figure 3.2. Becoming a master of one of these broad strategies will often mean that the library can differentiate itself from its competitors.

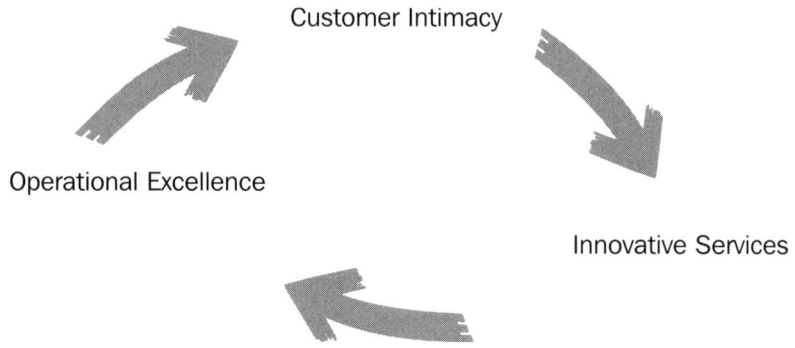

Figure 3.2. Interrelationship of Broad Strategies

Operational excellence focuses on providing customers with reliable products and services delivered with minimal inconvenience or difficulty. The customers of the library must make a conscious decision to visit the library (in-person or electronically) among the many options they have for obtaining the information that they are seeking. Dell Computers, Federal Express, and Wal-Mart are examples of companies that have focused on operational excellence. These companies are constantly seeking ways to minimize overhead costs, reduce transaction costs (including inconveniences), and eliminate departmental boundaries.

Customer intimacy focuses on targeting and segmenting markets with personalized offerings that match the needs of that particular niche. Using information freely provided by their customers, an organization will tailor its service and product offerings. Such tailoring might involve optional personalization services such as that found on Amazon.com or frequent buyer membership clubs to provide different levels of service to various segments of the marketplace.

Innovative services result from an organization clearly understanding the needs of its customers and finding ways to deliver higher levels of value. Organizations that focus on product or service leadership often do so by adapting ideas that they have "borrowed" from other organizations.

In support of these broad organizational strategies, a library can pursue technology-based strategies that complement the goals of the library. These technological strategies will range from the leading edge (some call this the bleeding edge) to laggards, as shown in Figure 3.3. For the libraries that have good financial support and flexibility in assigning resources, the library staff may wish to experiment with one or more new technologies that they hope will support an existing service or assist in developing a new service for the library's customers.

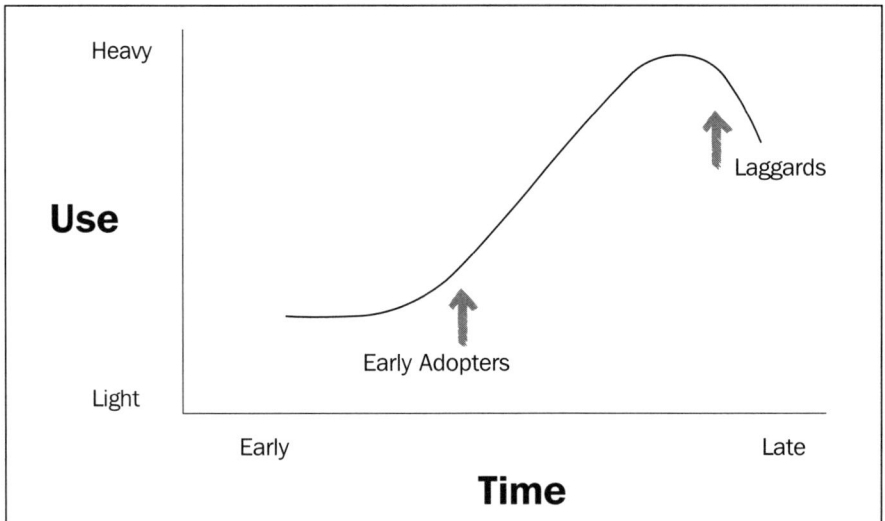

Figure 3.3. Technology Adoption Curve

For most libraries, the reality is that there is a total disconnect between the daily actions of managers and the activities of staff members and the library's mission statement and vision for the future. Strategy is not about destination but about the route the library chooses to take: *how* to reach the desired destination. Most important, an effective strategy is one that will differentiate the library from its competitors.

Preventing some of the more commonly made mistakes will allow the library to move from strategy formulation to implementation with relative ease. These mistakes include confusing strategies with goals that are derived from the library's vision; not developing the cause-and-effect relationships between strategies and the anticipated goals; failing to identify and implement performance measures that accurately measure the strategy; and not devoting sufficient time and resources to the training and instruction of all employees.[7]

At the conclusion of this phase of the planning process, the library should be able to answer seven key questions:

- *What* do we do?
- *Who* are we here for?
- What do our customers *want* and why?
- How can we better *improve* their satisfaction and the library's performance?
- What is the *strategy* and *process* for delivering library services?
- *What* needs to be done? *Who* will do it? *When*?
- Do we know or can we *determine* the library's contribution to and the impact of library services on the lives of its customers?

A sample of a section from a technology plan that focuses on the challenges facing a library follows.

Sample Section from a Technology Plan

Section 2: Challenges Facing the Library[8]

Mission Statement

The University Library connects students and scholars to the world of information and ideas. With a daily commitment to excellence and innovation, we select and create, organize and protect, provide and teach access to resources that are relevant to our campus programs and pursuits.

Proposed Technology Vision Statement

As one of the largest libraries in the United States, the University library will continue to be an innovator at the cutting edge in the use of digital technology for library purposes. The library will use technology not only to automate its current tasks but also to expand its reach and enhance the scholarly productivity of the university. The library will give students and professors immediate and effective access to information within the library collections and to the broader universe of information available via technology. Library staff will continue to have all training and talent necessary to use our information technology with ease and to teach patrons to become comfortable with the library systems.

Strengths, Weaknesses, Opportunities, and Threats

Introduction

The Strengths, Weaknesses, Opportunities, and Threats (SWOT) analysis surveys the status of the library from an internal and external perspective. The Strengths section focuses on the internal strengths of the library. The Weaknesses section focuses on the internal flaws of the institution. The Opportunities section looks at the external possibilities that the university library might help realize. It considers changes in the marketplace or in the political environment that the library might use to improve its service to its patrons. The Weaknesses section looks at the factors in the political and economic environment that might undermine the effectiveness of the library.

The TEMPLES (Technology, Economy, Markets, Politics, Law, Ethics, Society) acronym is used to specify areas of concern for the library. The sections below examine each of these areas.

Technology

Strengths: The library long has been at the cutting edge in its use of digital technology to promote its collections. Several of the collections at the library have been digitized, and the library has even begun to use its material as a source of revenue by selling prints and images. Because the university library is centrally located on campus, it is able to use the sophisticated network technology built by the campus and has access to network support from the campus technology office. The library also has been at the center of the campus's plan to provide wireless Internet access. Currently, three campus libraries including the main library provide wireless access. The library also will be updating its servers in the immediate future.

Weaknesses: The custom ALIS database used by the library is extremely old and lacks many of the features that librarians now expect in OPACs. It does not allow for acquisition or serials control, so that the library must use separate Innopac modules for these functions. This increases the costs of maintaining the systems and increases the costs of training employees. Nor does ALIS allow for Boolean searching or keyword searching. For example, it is not possible to search for a word or words in a title in ALIS. One must type in the exact beginning of the title to match the record. In 1995, the Library Systems Office (LSO) added DataFinder, which provided an HTTP interface and solved many of the searching problems. However, having two difference databases increases workload for the systems office, which loads all of the updates from ALIS to DataFinder each night. It also increases the complexity of staff work and training time because staff must use one database (ALIS) for maintenance and another (DataFinder) for searching and reference.

Opportunities: The increasing use of Open Systems may make it possible to add new systems without the costs associated with a vendor. Advances in standards such as Encoded Archival Description (EAD) may make it possible to standardize access to archival collections and increase our ability to preserve digital collections. E-publishing initiatives developed by the library may encourage more scholars to publish online and decrease the library's dependence on increasingly expensive journal publishers. Increasing penetration of broadband networks will make digital collections increasingly accessible to off-site users.

Threats: Growing use of Internet search engines for reference and information may make students less likely to use the library for research. Declining reference and circulation statistics due to the increasing use of online resources may make the library look less significant in the eyes of campus administrators. Increasing use of e-publishing by vendors may reduce the library's ability to own, preserve, and provide access to information. Publishers may force libraries to license instead of own the material that they publish. They also may come to see libraries as unnecessary middlemen if they can sell content directly to Internet users at home. The increasing prevalence of computer viruses also may endanger library systems.

Economy

Strengths: During the 1990s, the acquisitions budget for new materials was increased significantly.

Weaknesses: The library was weakened significantly by the state recession in the early 1990s and did not fully recover in the boom of the late 1990s. Staff salaries for librarians and especially for library assistants have lagged behind market rates, according to university studies. Low salaries, especially when combined with the high cost of housing, have made it extremely difficult for the library to attract talented employees from other areas.

Opportunities: None . . . one can pray that the state budget has reached is nadir and soon will rebound. Current high rates of unemployment will make it easier to recruit talented employees when and if the library has money to hire people. Computer equipment prices have fallen as the hardware has become standardized. There is some evidence (the growing use of Linux) that software prices also will decline due to the increasing use of open standards.

Threats: Library budgets were cut by 10 percent last year, and the campus asked library administrators to prepare for a possible 20 percent cut next year. There is no obvious end in sight to the current state recession. The state budget crisis, which usually lags a year or two behind the start and end of economic recessions, probably will last even longer than the recession.

Markets

Strengths: The library has one of the largest and most diverse research collections in the United States. The library also has unique resources and extensive collections representing several areas from around the world.

Weaknesses: The library needs to better understand its users and their needs. An analysis of interlibrary loan borrowing should be done as well as performing a survey of users to determine whether they are finding what they are looking for (the survey might be split into two groups: those that visit the library and those that access the information resources online from outside the library).

Opportunities: The university library has begun to sell some of its unique digital material on the Internet. If this project is successful, it can be expanded to include other materials housed in the library. Growing use of electronic journals may reduce the price of serials acquisitions. The library's project to publish scholarly articles on its own servers may improve its bargaining position with respect to publishers.

Threats: The price of science periodicals still is out of control. Between 1986 and 2000 the cost of scholarly journals increased by 227 percent, four times the rate of inflation. The current costs for commercial OPACs may be prohibitive for the library with its current budget. There is a possibility that the spread of large comfortable bookstores, such as Barnes and Noble, may make university libraries less attractive locations for browsing and studying.

Politics

Strengths: The current university librarian generally has the respect and trust of the staff.

Weaknesses: Currently, due to the new budget crisis in the state, the library has a hiring freeze. The library administration hopes that the hiring freeze will make layoffs unnecessary. However, the policy leads to cannibalization and competition between library departments. When an employee leaves the library, the unit that loses the employee either must either accept a vacancy or convince the administration that its work is important enough so that it can recruit an employee from another unit within the library.

Opportunities: It is unlikely that the state voters knowingly will allow the university system, which gives them the opportunity to receive relatively cheap education, to decline. Library and university administrators can use this popular support to push for increased funding.

Threats: Support for education among voters is counterbalanced by distaste for taxes. Consequently, funding for the university often has been decreased in recent years. The economic polarization of the state (the decline of the middle class and the growth of the rich and the poor in recent years) also tends to reduce support for the university. The poor usually do not see the university as an educational option, and the rich, who can afford any private university, do not see the need for a publicly supported university.

Law

Strengths: The change in tax law in the 1990s regarding the inventory tax for publishers means that an item more than two to three years old is difficult to acquire.

Weaknesses: Nationally, recent changes that strengthen the copyright laws tend to favor publishers over libraries.

Opportunities: The American Library Association (ALA) and the Association of Research Libraries (ARL) continue to advocate in favor of library issues on a national basis. The university library can use its connections with these organizations to promote its own legal interests.

Threats: Increased copyright protections will make it harder to digitize collections and may make the library vulnerable to copyright lawsuits. Also, music companies that try to prosecute patrons and employees who download music using library servers may endanger the library. The new powers of the Patriot Act may decrease the privacy of library patrons.

Ethics

Strengths: Most library employees are dedicated to the mission of the library.

Weaknesses: The occasional gossip among some library employees about the dress and behavior of some library users should be addressed.

Opportunities: We can expect to continue to take advantage of the general honesty of our patrons and staff to maintain our collections.

Threats: Low staff morale due to low wages may encourage reduced performance or even occasional sabotage. Lack of staff in the new stacks makes adding PCs to these areas a security risk and compels the continued use of dummy terminals.

Society

Strengths: The library staff is very large and highly qualified. There are a large group of experienced librarians and library assistants working in all areas of library services. The library has a significant amount of programming talent working on its databases, servers, and digital collections. The library also has access to a talented and intelligent student body, from which it can recruit for temporary, part-time employment. The current university librarian and the library administration have been very proactive and effective at making sure that the campus maintains its commitment to the library's technology needs and its collection.

Weaknesses: Staff morale also has been low since the 1990s, and there has been a significant amount of labor tension. Library assistants, who belong to the university's clerical union, went on a three-day strike at the beginning of the 2002 academic year to protest low wages and apparent university indifference to their plight.

Opportunities: Most Americans continue to see libraries as vital public institutions. Despite the worries of some library professionals, few citizens believe that the emergence of the Internet is making libraries less important. There also continues to be strong support for public education.

Threats: The belief that everything useful can be or should be online may make it more difficult to support the continued development of the physical collections of the library, especially the unique manuscript and rare book collections at the university library. Continuing fears of increased terrorism may strengthen support for the Patriot Act and other laws that reduce the privacy of library patrons. The growing faith in privatization and market-based solutions to social problems may reduce support for publicly funded institutions such as the university library.

Conclusion

The greatest priority for the library is its need for an improved OPAC. However, due to the economic weakness of the library, it is unlikely that the library will be able to purchase a commercial system in the near future.

Notes

1. From *Bartlett's Familiar Quotations,* 16th ed., Justin Kaplan, general editor (Boston: Little, Brown, 1992).

2. Nils-Goran Olve, Jan Roy, and Magnus Wetter. *Performance Drivers: A Practical Guide to Using the Balanced Scorecard.* New York, Wiley, 1999.

3. Simon Wootton and Terry Horne. *Strategic Thinking: A Step-by-Step Approach to Strategy.* Dover, NH: Kogan Page, 2000.

4. Brook E. Sheldon. Strategic Planning for Public Library Services in the 21st Century. *Managing Public Libraries in the 21st Century,* 1989, 199–208.

5. Andrew Campbell and Marcus Alexander. What's Wrong with Strategy? *Harvard Business Review*, 75 (6), November–December 1997, 42–51.

6. Michael Treacy and Fred Wiersema. Customer Intimacy and Other Value Disciplines. *Harvard Business Review*, 71 (1), January/February 1993, 84–93.

7. Heather Johnson. Strategic Planning for Modern Libraries. *Library Management*, 15 (1), 1994, 7–18.

8. John Wenzler prepared this sample section of a technology plan.

Emerging Technologies

> *Technology . . . is the knack of so arranging the world that we don't have to experience it.*—Max Frisch[1]

Quite clearly one of the constants in the technology arena is that change is constant. Existing technology is evolving and improving while new technologies are being adopted in the marketplace. It is also important to note that as newly emerging technologies become widely accepted, they will likely be replaced by even newer emerging technologies. A great deal of the new technology is being developed outside the realm of libraries, but it will likely have a major impact on the way libraries are able to deliver services and information to the library customer, wherever the customer is located. Thus, library staff need to recognize that some of these technology trends will likely affect libraries in the not too distant future.

One of the challenges is to attempt to identify the more significant technologies that will have an impact on libraries, especially those that will become a force in the marketplace over the next three to five years. Attempting to do this on a systematic basis can be a daunting task. Reading publications outside the library field and visiting some of the technology-oriented Web sites will help the librarian see technology from a broader perspective. Connecting with people at conferences and chatting with like-minded colleagues are two effective strategies. Ultimately, no matter how "sexy and fun" a new technology may be, the fundamental question to ask is, how will the use of any particular technology add to the library's ability to provide value to its customers?

Some medical libraries have been able to successfully embrace new technologies without encountering too many implementation problems. And, of course, two Internet-based companies that should be carefully monitored to see what is new that might be emulated within a library are Google and Amazon.com.

Given the pervasive adoption of the Internet, the Internet itself is not considered as a trend but rather as a reality that the vast majority of libraries today are using in some manner. The uses of the Internet may be thought of as a pipeline to deliver messages and information. The World Wide Web or "the Web" may be referred to as the content side of the equation. A Web site may be used as a search engine to find other helpful Web sites and documents, as well as for a myriad of other uses. In fact, anticipating the uses to which the Web can be put is a good planning strategy. Internet2, for example, is a BIG pipe and a trend worth watching.

The following seven technologies are presented in no particular order—all deserve to be watched and considered by library managers, decision makers, and interested professional librarians. After all, it is likely that these technologies will have an impact on the library in the not too distant future. It is probable that, in any given year, new technologies can be added to this list.

Among the technologies that a library might want to monitor are

- TCP/IP everywhere,
- Peer-to-peer networking,
- XML,
- Wireless connections,
- Voice and translation capabilities,
- Web services, and
- RFID.

TCP/IP Everywhere

The number of people connecting to the Internet will continue to increase for the foreseeable future, but there will come a time when the pace of adoption will decline. However, this will not mean that the Internet will see a decline in usage. In computer chip technology, a phenomenon known as "Moore's Law" states that the number of components on computer chips doubles every 18 months, while price remains constant. As the volume of production increases, the costs for a computer chip will decline over time.

The implication of Moore's Law is that not only does the price/performance of computer systems continue to improve each year, but these increasingly more powerful computer chips are being embedded in a host of other products. These products range from handheld personal digital assistants, to cellular phones enabled to interact with the Internet, to pagers and other "net appliances," to the chips being embedded in automobiles, vending machines, household appliances, clothing, and so forth.

Feedback loops are incorporated into the Net so that existing products and services can be improved. Kevin Kelly calls these feedback loops "virtuous circles."[2] The virtuous circles feed upon themselves, so that prices decline and quality improves significantly over time.

The glue that makes it possible to connect all of these devices to the Internet is Transmission Control Protocol/Internet Protocol (TCP/IP) communications software. We are seeing TCP/IP being used to provide telephone services via the Net (called telephony), desktop videoconferencing, broadcast of audio and video, and much more. The reason for all of this activity is that using TCP/IP significantly decreases complexity and therefore the cost of providing a particular service. Having one network communication protocol means that from anything, you can talk to anything.

Metcalfe's Law, which indicates that the value of a network increases exponentially as more participants are included, results in what is sometimes called the "network effect"—value rises exponentially with market share. Today, because an increasing number of people are linked via the Internet, more goods and services gain their value from this widespread network effect.

One of the implications of making connections to all of these devices is that a wide range of services is now available without regard to distance. No longer is it necessary to visit a bank branch, physically be present to attend a university, call a broker to execute a stock transaction, or go someplace to obtain a cost quote, product, or service. All of this and more, much more, is now be accomplished using the Internet. The consequences of this for a library is that it must consider and identify ways that it can provide some or all of its services without requiring the customer to physically visit the library. Whether through document delivery, online 24/7 reference services, borrowing of materials, or providing access to online databases, libraries must change the way they provide services.

Access to the Internet means that a host of library competitors have been developed and will continue to arise. The challenge for any library is to determine how it can increase the value offered customers so that the library remains a vital place in the lives of people.

Peer-to-Peer Networking

The essential idea behind peer-to-peer (P2P) networking is simplicity itself: You share files and programs and computer processing cycles and communicate directly with other people over a local area network (LAN) and/or the Internet without having to rely on a centralized server. The end result is the prospect of distributed file systems, distributed search engines, virtual supercomputers, and so much more.[3] This idea can be and has been applied in a number of interesting ways ranging from the sharing of files, to collaborative software using a shared workspace, to sharing of "idle" computer processing cycles, and so forth. If you have used instant messaging you have used a P2P program. The whole idea of P2P software is to eliminate the middleman (the server on the network).

Peer-to-peer computing differs from client/server in three fundamental ways:

- In P2P processing the exchange of services is symmetric (that is, it is happening between peers running identical software and having roughly the same processing power) and each computer has equivalent responsibility.

- In client/server, there is a one-to-many relationship—one server supports many clients. In P2P processing, there are any number of cooperating peers, any of which can initiate an interaction or transaction with another peer.

- The client/server interaction has a fixed capacity, while P2P provides transparent access to services of any kind with an almost unlimited capacity.

P2P collaborative software allows an individual to share information and documents with selected other individuals within an organization, across an entire organization, or with outside groups. This approach has the potential for significantly improving the productivity among employees within an organization. One company attracting considerable attention with P2P collaborative software is Groove Networks. Such software allows for the routing of documents, electronically annotating one another's work, viewing ideas on a white board, having online discussions, and so forth. Any work done offline is immediately shared and updated as soon as you connect to the network.

In addition to improving personal productivity, P2P computing offers the opportunity for reducing centralized computer resources and eliminating redundant computer storage. Such an approach takes advantage of the unused processing power and disk storage space on each desktop workstation. Imagine the number of e-mails, often with attachments, and their associated storage space, that have been forwarded, saved, and then forwarded again. Not only do P2P software solutions keep track of files across an organization's entire network, they offer interesting possibilities for searching and indexing documents and other files that exist on the desktop workstations of individuals within an organization.

P2P search engines offer the prospect of utilizing metadata, for example the XML-based Dublin Core, in describing and classifying information to be found at a Web site. The Dublin Core, combined with the Resource Description Framework (RDF), a data model and XML serialization syntax for describing resources, means that new approaches can be used to overcome the serious limitations of the existing Web search engines.

P2P systems will likely raise some interesting issues. Among these are the following:

- Who owns a document or other work that has been created and enhanced through the collaborative process?
- How do you exert leadership in a peer-to-peer world?
- How will values within an organization change in a peer-to-peer world? Currently, some people within an organization retain their value by being an "expert" in a subject area. In some cases, this same individual also exercises control by being a gatekeeper and determining when and with whom information is shared.
- The peer-to-peer world seems to blur the distinction between the workspace and personal space.

XML

Extensible Markup Language (XML), designed specifically for the Web, is a simpler version of the original and more complex Standard Generalized Markup Language (SGML). Organizations can define, transmit, validate, and interpret data between applications and databases. XML provides structure rather than being a presentation system. XML separates the underlying data from how the data are displayed; thus the data can more easily be organized, programmed, edited, and exchanged between Web sites and applications. XML and its associated Data Type Definition or DTD (gradually being replaced by the XSD described below) play an important role in the exchange of information. In addition to the rules for establishing XML entities, there are nine other key XML-related standards. Two of the more important of these standards are described below.

- **XML Schema Definition (XSD)** defines a consistent way of describing XML document structures and adding data types to XML data fields. The intent of this standard is to facilitate cross-organizational document exchange and verification. Tools are available for converting XML DTDs (Document Type Definitions) to XSD that assist in the exchange of information.
- **Simple Object Access Protocol (SOAP)** is one of the more popular XML Schema Definitions that allows applications to pass data and instructions to one another. SOAP was originally developed for distributed applications to communicate over Hypertext Transfer Protocol (HTTP) and through firewalls. SOAP defines the use of XML and HTTP to access services, objects, and servers in a platform-independent manner. SOAP does not define any application semantics

such as a programming model or implementation-specific semantics; rather, it defines a simple mechanism for expressing application semantics by providing a modular packaging model and encoding mechanisms for encoding data within modules. This allows SOAP to be used in a large variety of systems ranging from messaging systems to a remote procedure call.

The Book Industry Standards Advisory Committee (BISAC) and the Serials Industry Standards Advisory Committee (SISAC) are developing XSDs to facilitate ordering, acknowledging receipt of an order, claiming, and other transaction sets. Once adopted as standards by the National Information Standards Organization, these XSDs will be incorporated into applications by both the library information system vendors and the book and serials jobbers.

Resource Description Framework (RDF) is an XML-based infrastructure that enables the encoding, exchange, and reuse of structured metadata. RDF allows for more than one type of data to be included in the same metadata package. A group of interested parties is working on representing the Dublin Core in RDF.

OCLC and the RLG are in the process of implementing new systems that will store bibliographic and other data as XML rather than using the traditional MARC structures. Software programs will convert the data into the format desired by the customer. Also worth mentioning are the various XML-MARC implementations and MODS, a simple MARC that is consistent with XML. Both indicate the growing importance to libraries of XML.

Wireless Connections

The growth of the wireless industry has been truly amazing. In 1999, there were some 469 million wireless subscribers worldwide and by the end of 2004, this number will have reached some 1.6+ billion wireless subscribers.

The first- and second-generation wireless protocols are designed for voice-only communications, while the third-generation protocol is designed for both voice and data. Due to the high costs of implementation, it is anticipated that third-generation digital-based services will be slow to arrive. Existing wireless technologies will be used to deliver services for the foreseeable future. In Japan, a popular second-generation service called I-mode or DoCoMo offers low-cost instant messaging and limited Internet services from I-mode enabled cellular phones. This service is particularly attractive to students, parents, and businessmen.

The emerging family of standards for wireless is IEEE 802.11. This group of standards allows a library to implement wireless services within a library so that library customers can gain access to the library's OPAC from their personal digital assistants (PDAs) or laptops. 802.11b is sometimes referred to as wireless fidelity or Wi-Fi. Obviously the library's automated information system must be able to support Wi-Fi communications. A 802.11 node or base station can be implemented for a relatively small expense and supports communication with devices up to 300 feet away.

Other libraries are implementing Bluetooth nodes so that individuals with Bluetooth-enabled devices (typically PDAs and cell phones) can "synch up" and communicate with one another using text-based messages. Bluetooth is not compatible with an 802.11 network.

Libraries might also want to consider use of wireless barcode scanners in lieu of scanners at a desktop that use a data cable, or using a wireless barcode scanner when a service line becomes too long.

Voice and Translation Capabilities

Speech recognition is actually a combination of computer hardware and software that recognizes spoken words. Today's voice recognition systems allow the individual to speak naturally and usually do not require the user to "teach" the system how to recognize his or her voice. Such systems are useful in instances when the user is unable to use a keyboard to enter data or the individual has a low typing speed.

Even though speech recognition software is now about 97 percent effective—that is, the system correctly recognizes and displays the spoken words in text form on the screen—that still means that three words in a hundred or three words in 10 lines of text would need to have the "typos" corrected by the individual. Fortunately, the spell-checking feature of most word processing applications will assist in this process. Over time, speech recognition systems will continue to improve so that the individual can speak at a faster rate with fewer associated typos.

Voice-based browser technology is promising full-fledged voice access to Internet. VoiceXML 2.0, a draft standard being worked on by the World Wide Web Consortium (W3C), is a standard markup language for voice data that will provide a common means for integrating touch pad signals, synthesized speech, and speech recognition within a Web-based application. Already there are Web sites that will translate a Web page from one language to another.

One of the by-products of computer-telephony integration is that TCP/IP will be used to place phone calls, deliver a fax, etc. This capability is sometimes called Voice Over Internet Protocol (VOIP). Some organizations with remote offices and facilities have significantly reduced their telephone bills by using VOIP to handle voice communications using the Internet "pipe" to handle the calls.

Web Services

As more and more business is conducted over the Internet, organizations face the problem of making their applications work with those of their suppliers and customers. This process of having applications communicate with one another is often called systems integration.

There are several approaches to integration, but they can be grouped into three categories, discussed below.

Custom Integration

The two parties agree on a communications standard or protocol, write any needed data conversions, and the two applications are linked. The obvious problem with this approach is that as the number of applications or partners increase, the number of possible data protocols and "custom" data conversions begins to increase—seemingly at an exponential rate. Clearly this is an expensive process for all partners.

Middleware Product

The organization could purchase a "middleware product," which establishes a common communications standard. The organization simply writes a data conversion routine (software program) for each application it wishes to integrate. The problems with this approach are threefold: First, the middleware software is not inexpensive; second, the organization must have, or contract to an outside third party, the necessary computer programming resources to create and maintain these data conversion programs; and third, the organization must convince each of its customers and/or suppliers to adopt the same middleware software product.

Web Services

Web services are applications that have been enabled to use a standard universal language to send data and instructions to one another, with no data translation or conversion required. And since the Internet is being used, the connection problems are minimized or eliminated. To date, most data and information accessible via the Internet are viewed by people using a browser, and thus the Net can be thought of as "people-centric." To be used by an application within an organization the information must be either "scraped" from the screen or sent by the information supplier (the variety of nonstandard formats depends upon the number of information suppliers).

Rather than relying on the brute-force, custom approach or using proprietary middleware software, Web services rely on an open, standards-based approach that, at least in theory, obviates the disadvantages of the first two options. Examples of a Web service include:

- A credit checking service that returns credit information when given a person's social security number.

- A purchasing service that allows a computer system to buy office supplies when given an item code and a quantity.

- A stock quote service that returns the latest sock price associated with a particular ticker symbol.

Let's consider a library that wishes to place an order for several books. The library may enter the information into an acquisitions module that is a part of its library information system. The library information system will then send the order electronically using an electronic data interchange or electronic data interchange (EDI) protocol to the vendor of choice. Alternatively, the library staff can connect to several vendor Web sites to discover the pricing and availability of the items they wish to order—a fairly time-consuming process.

Using Web services, a different approach would be taken. The automated library information system vendors could set up a Web services-based price/availability comparison shopping option within the acquisitions module. This optional comparison-shopping feature would then automatically check with a number of vendors about price/availability for the items of interest. The results would then be displayed for the library to make a decision about where to place the order.

Web services are likely to be at the heart of the next generation of distributed services. Here's why:

- **The Internet:** The Internet is a way in which various applications and services are linked—and almost every library and organization is linked to the Net.

- **Interoperability:** Any Web service can interact with any other Web service. Web services can run on any platform and be written in any programming language.

- **Low barrier to entry:** The concepts behind Web services are easy to understand. They offer a more flexible or "loosely coupled" way of linking applications. In addition, free toolkits are being provided by a host of vendors that allow developers to more quickly develop and deploy Web services. Web services are a way to link existing applications rather than requiring new software development for a complete module.

- **Ubiquity:** Since Web services rely on HTTP and XML, any device that supports these technologies can both host and access Web services. Even wireless services can be provided using Web services.

- **Industry support:** All of the major software vendors are supporting and are involved with extending the standards around which Web services are being built.

The book or serial vendor would verify the accuracy of the information using authentication procedures through passwords, public keys, or some other mechanism. The vendor may extend to the library a higher than normal discount due to the amount of prior spending or the presence of a contractual agreement between the vendor and the library.

One of the interesting side effects of Web services is that the range of services can be extended beyond the simple sending and receiving of EDI-based messages. After the order has been placed, the acquisitions module could automatically search for and download a cataloging record (MARC or XML or . . .). Once the library has received the order and invoice, the module could automatically update the library's parent organization's accounting system to show that funds have been expended and the book or serial vendor should be paid. What new, unforeseen applications will emerge when applications can interact with other applications—regardless of machine, operating system, programming language, or middleware?

There are, however, some issues that must be addressed before Web services become more popular. These issues include the following:

- **Reliability:** Some Web services will, inevitably, be more reliable than others. What happens when a Web service is unavailable for some period of time?

- **Security:** Will the Web service use encryption plus authentication to improve the level of security? Will the authentication process identify the required level of security for a transaction to occur?

- **Transactions:** In a closed, client/server-based system, a transaction is performed once the appropriate records have been "locked" so that another transaction does not alter the record or data field until the original transaction is completed. Such an approach will not work using Web services since transactions may span minutes, hours, or even days.

- **Scalability:** Supporting distributed Web services will require system monitoring tools to make sure that the system can support the volume of transactions, recognizing that there will be peaks and valleys of demand.

- **Accountability:** How are users of Web services charged? How long can a user use a Web service for a specific price?
- **Testing:** When a system is composed of many Web services whose locations are distributed, potentially across thousands of miles, testing and debugging become even more challenging. Will Web services be quality assured and certified?

RFID

Radio Frequency Identification or RFID combines computer chips with a very small radio. When this chip is "energized" by another radio signal, it will broadcast the information encoded on the computer chip. Such information might range from an identification number to other associated item identification information. The combination of the chips and radio is sometimes called "tags."

Grocery markets and retail stores are particularly interested in RFID, and as the price of a tag falls into the pennies per tag price range (as the manufacturing volume of the tags increases, the price will decrease), then a wide variety of applications will open up. For libraries, this may mean that a library could be open 24 hours a day and that items removed from the library would automatically be charged out to the person borrowing the items (assuming the individual also has an RFID as a part of his or her library card or organizational ID card). It may also mean that staffing for a circulation desk could be reduced, perhaps dramatically.

The Cerritos (California) Public Library, the Santa Clara (California) Public Library, the Chandler (Arizona) Public Library, the Maricopa County (Arizona) Public Library, the Orange County (Florida) Public Library, Providence (Rhode Island) College, and the University of Nevada at Las Vegas Library are already experimenting with RFID technology.

Summary

Once one or two particular technologies have been identified as having some potential, the role this technology can play in improving an existing library service or in introducing a new service should be considered. Most important, the potential impact on the library's customers should be addressed. Only if the library can answer affirmatively that the proposed technology will add value from the customer's perspective should the library move to planning for implementation.

Notes

1. Max Frisch. *Homo Faber*, 1957. From *Bartlett's Familiar Quotations,* 16th ed., Justin Kaplan, general editor (Boston: Little, Brown, 1992).

2. Kevin Kelly. *New Rules for the New Economy: 10 Radical Strategies for a Connected World.* New York: Viking, 1998.

3. Andy Oram (Editor). *Peer-to-Peer: Harnessing the Benefits of a Disruptive Technology.* Cambridge, MA: O'Reilly, 2001.

Current Technology Environment

> *Any sufficiently advanced technology is indistinguishable from magic.*—Arthur Clarke[1]

This section of the technology plan contains a description of the current technology environment of the library. In short, this step in the preparation of a technology plan can be thought of as "taking inventory." It will certainly be easier the second time around but can be difficult the first time when it may be necessary to contact a number of individuals within the library and perhaps individuals from other outside departments or organizations to obtain the information necessary to complete this section of the plan. For example, it may be necessary to contact a city/county or campus information technology department and the library's Internet service provider (ISP), among others.

An inventory of equipment, software, cabling, and staffing resources devoted to implementing and supporting technology within the library should be prepared, or if one already exists, it should be checked and updated as needed. Technologies that might be included in such an inventory are shown in Table 5.1.

Table 5.1. Possible Technologies to Be Included in a Plan

General Technologies

Telephone system
Fax machines
Materials security system
Photocopiers (black and white, color)
Microfilm viewers, printers
Typewriters

Information Technology

Internet connection
Wide area network
Local area network
Servers
Desktop computers
Dumb terminals
Printers
Image scanners (save an image file, convert to text)
Barcode scanners
Wireless network

Audio and Video

Television
VCR player
DVD player
Cassette player
Headphones

ADA Equipment

Screen enlarger
Text to speech converter
Text to Braille converter

This inventory should include information about the purpose, quantity, age, brand, capacity, version or release number, and other characteristics of the following:

- **Physical facilities:** Within the context of technology, the ready availability of conduits for data cables and electrical outlets to plug in the various pieces of equipment should be noted.

- **Network infrastructure:** The description of the network infrastructure should identify the network typology (bus, ring, or star), type of cabling, along with the actual and potential bandwidth of the network.

Connections from the library to the Internet should be identified. A network diagram would be helpful, along with a description of the link to the Internet. If the library supports a wireless network so that library customers can gain access to the library's OPAC and/or other services, this network should also be described.

- **Network:** Reliability, network response times (average and during peak periods of use), volume of traffic, etc. Often this information can be best presented using graphs, but the important points should be described in the narrative.
- **Computer hardware/operating system—servers:** The information about the computer hardware can be presented in a table. A short table, as shown in Table 5.2, can summarize the information. It is not necessary to include the complete inventory in the technology plan itself.
- **Computer hardware/operating system—desktops:** A description of the desktop workstations, similar to the servers, should be included.
- **Software applications—library information system:** This narrative should include information about when the system was purchased, name of the vendor providing and supporting the system, modules being used, the release of the software currently installed, the anticipated date for the installation of the next release of the software, and a sense of the overall satisfaction in using this software.
- **Software applications—librarywide:** This description should include information about what software applications are used to support the operation of the library. Such software packages might include accounting, payroll, personnel management, physical assets inventory, and so forth. Information about each application should identify the name of the vendor, release of the software currently installed, date first installed, etc.
- **Software applications—desktops:** This narrative should describe what software is installed on staff and public access workstations. Such software might include office productivity packages such as MS Office, an Internet browser, Java, antivirus software, and much more. As noted above, information about each application should identify the name of the vendor, release of the software currently installed, date first installed, etc.

- **Technical support:** This narrative should describe how two groups of people will be able to receive support should they encounter problems while attempting to use technology. These two groups are library staff members and the library's customers.
    - Customers: What do customers do when they encounter a problem while using the library's OPAC, trying to print, or on the Internet? Are staff trained to provide assistance? Are there limits to providing assistance?
    - Library staff members: Is a specific staff member or group of staff charged with the responsibility of maintaining the network and providing troubleshooting assistance when a problem is encountered or the network goes down?
- **Data—backups, virus protection:** Procedures for backups, answering the following questions: How frequently are backups of various data files and software programs made? Where are these backup files kept? How are data files and software programs protected from computer viruses? How frequently is the virus protection software updated? A library spends a considerable amount of time and other resources in creating and maintaining a number of data files, for example, patron, bibliographic, and authority records. It is essential that the library define and periodically test and update a sound backup plan.
- **Staff skills:** Are staff comfortable and knowledgeable about the use of all of the technologies to be found in the library? Are training classes routinely offered for staff to improve their skills? Do staff members consider themselves to be beginners, about average, or expert users when it comes to
    - the operating system (Windows, Unix, and so forth),
    - Web-browser skills (functions available when using a browser),
    - Internet searching skills,
    - commercial application software skills (MS Office), and
    - library application specific skills?

Table 5.2. Sample Summary Table of Equipment

Location/ Purpose	Quantity	Date Purchased	Brand	Characteristics	Operating System
Staff Technical Services Workstations	45	2000	Dell OptiPlex with a 15-inch "boxy" monitor	512 MB of RAM memory, 40 MG of disk space, CD ROM read/write drive, 100/100 Mbps NIC card	Windows 98
Online Public Access Catalogs	30	2001	Dell OptiPlex with a 17-inch flat screen monitor	256 MB of RAM memory, 20 MG of disk space, 100/100 Mbps NIC card	Windows 2000

In addition to the information technology-related hardware and software, the narrative should also identify other equipment in the library. Such equipment might include microfilm readers and printers, photocopiers, audio players and headsets, video players and monitors, and equipment and software to facilitate access for people with disabilities to conform to the Americans with Disabilities Act (ADA).

Depending upon the age of the library's telephone system, the library may wish to examine the possibility that its telephone system should be replaced or upgraded, and it should be included in the description of the current environment.

The sample section of a technology plan presented below follows the structure discussed in this chapter.

Sample Section from a Technology Plan

Current Technology Environment[2]

LAN Network

The current local area network (LAN) at the Martinez location is a star topology consisting of a Dell PowerEdge 2600 server (purchased in 2003),

WatchGuard Firebox SOHO6tc, Cat 5e twisted-pair wiring and a 24-port patch panel, Cisco Catalyst 2924 XL switch, and a DSL Cayman Router. The Dell server is running Windows 2000. The staff is linked to Contra Costa County's server for e-mail and Internet access via a T-1 line. The speed of our LAN is 100.0 Mbps. The public access terminals connect to the Internet through a SBC DSL line with a speed of 6 Mbps.

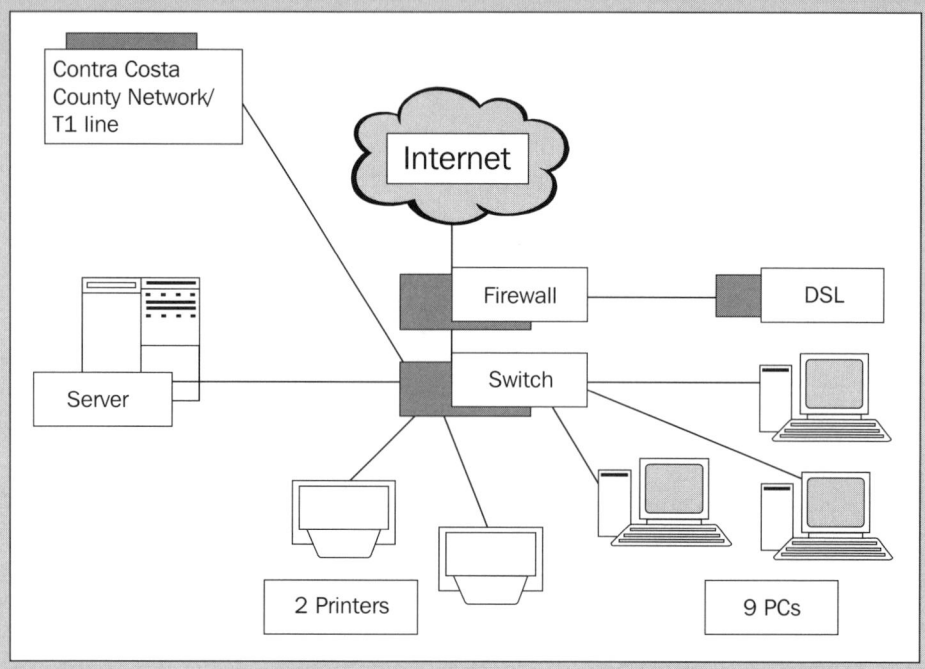

The Veritas Backup Exec software automatically backs up the network resources weekly and a staff member rotates the tapes.

Symantec's Antivirus Corporate Edition version 8 protects the library system and it is configured for weekly automatic updates for the network, staff workstations, and public workstations. The Richmond location has access to the Library's LAN through a VPN connection. The Richmond location has a firewall (SOHO Watchguard) with virus protection for both the staff and public computers. (Critique: Does the library have a plan to respond to a virus "takeover" of its system? How likely is such an event? Has a virus affected the computers in the library in the last two years?)

Contra Costa County (California) Department of Information Technology (DOIT) installed Category 5 cabling in early 1997 throughout the library to connect the PC workstations and printers to the LAN at the Martinez location. The

Martinez library building is capable of supporting the existing electrical demands of the library's technology equipment; however, the same was not true for the Richmond location. The Richmond location was updated in 2003 for additional electrical and high-speed line connections for phones, computers, and Internet access.

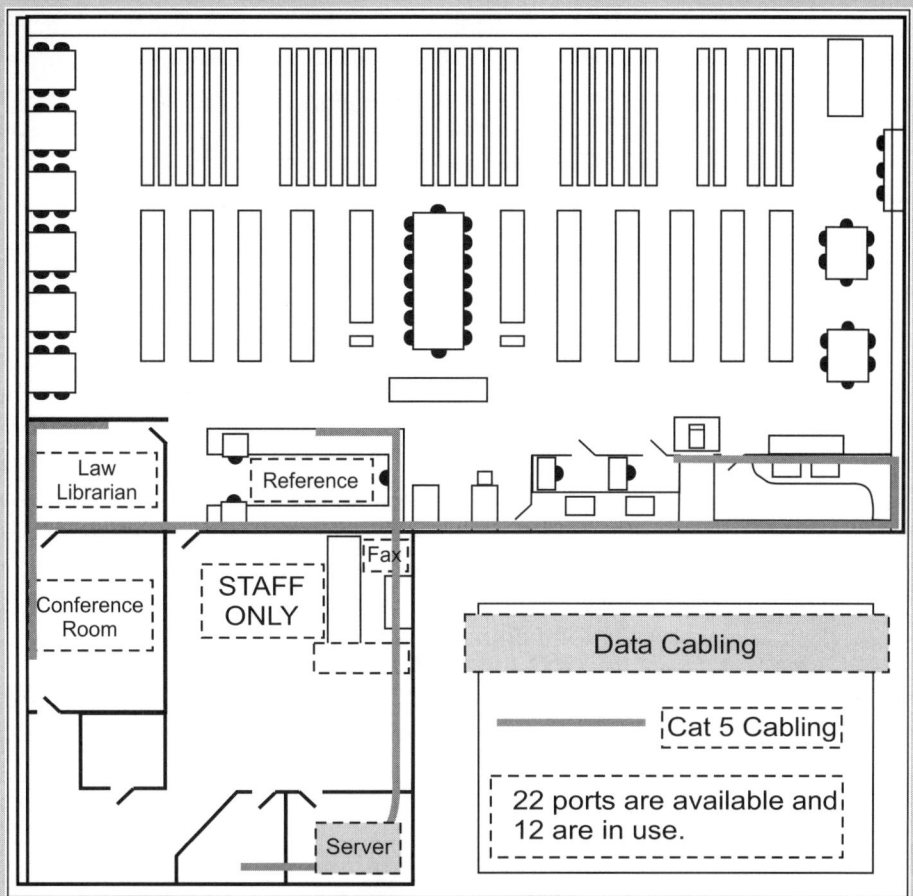

Telecommunications Services

Local telephone service is provided via Contra Costa County's telecom system. The library is billed monthly by the Department of Information Technology for our phone usage. The SBC DSL connection is also billed through the County's IT Department. The county provides support for our DSL line. An annual estimate of our communication budget requirements is determined by the Department of Information Technology and sent to the library for review early in the year.

Library Catalog System

The library's Web Online Public Access Catalog (OPAC) is one of the SydneyPlus modules of an integrated library system that was purchased in 1996. The library also utilizes the standard catalog, serials, and report writing modules of the SydneyPlus system. The "acquisitions" module was purchased in 1996 as well, but the library staff has not used it.

The library tested and installed the Web version of SydneyPlus's Online Public Access Catalog in late 2002. It had been purchased three years before and was returned to the vendor when the library was unsuccessful in making it work with our Internet vendor. Since that time, the library has changed Internet vendors and SydneyPlus felt that they had worked out most of the issues with this product. The OPAC tested as satisfactory (not perfect), and the library is currently paying the $12,000 for this new module through this fiscal year.

SydneyPlus has started converting their library systems product to an SQL platform this year. All clients will have to move to this platform eventually (they state within a year) since they will no longer support the older platform.

We will have a year to review their new product and determine whether we want to remain with this vendor. If we decide to remain with SydneyPlus, the current software will have to be upgraded to the new SQL version, which will involve additional software, hardware, and technical support expenditures. In addition to the SQL Server hardware and software, as well as the SQL client licenses, a staff member will have to be trained to administer the new SQL Server. We currently pay SydneyPlus $8,000 annually for upgrades, maintenance, and support.

Workstation Operating Software

The staff's five Dell 8200 workstations have MS Windows 2000 Professional as a platform, Office XP Small Business (2002), Symantec's Antivirus Corporate Edition 8.17, and MS Internet Explorer version 6.0. All of the staff's computers have the Dell three-year extended warranty and service contract, which expires 10/03/04. Two of the workstations have additional software, one has Access 2001 and QuickBooks Pro installed, whereas the other has Adobe PhotoShop 5.0 and Netscape.

Our patrons have access to three Micron ClientPro CR PCs with MS Windows 2000 Professional as an operating system, Microsoft Windows XP Professional, WordPerfect 2000, and Symantec Antivirus Corporate Edition, which is managed at the server level. These three computers have a three-year maintenance warranty (expires 6/13/05).

The patrons also have access to our online catalog, CD-ROMs that accompany books, word processing, and Internet access (limited to three workstations). There are two stand-alone HP VectraVL Series PCs, with Windows 95, which are also available to the public for just word processing. These two computers have had performance issues, and we can only use them for word processing capabilities with outdated software.

Another HP VectraVL computer has been dedicated as our library's "online catalog" computer. Unfortunately, it is slow and the online catalog takes quite awhile to respond to any queries. People prefer the library catalog, which is on the Internet, to this older version.

CD-ROM Information Resources

All of the subscription CD-ROM services have been canceled since we had issues with the CD-ROM server. We also have found that the publishers are moving toward online resources that utilize the Internet. Some publishers still provide forms, etc. on CD-ROMs, which accompany their books. The online resources are favored over the CD-ROMs because there is no server maintenance and they are kept current by the vendor. The only issue is the learning curve for the staff and our patrons.

The rack that the CD-ROM server is currently housed in can be used for expansions to our present arrangement.

Licensed Online Services

In June 2002, the library signed licensed online licensing agreements with both LEXIS and Westlaw for just their California libraries, Shepards, a couple of popular treatises that we formerly had in CD-ROM format, as well as some forms packages. All of these products are accessed over the Internet using passwords to authenticate licensed users to the subscribed databases.

In late 2002, the library added another licensed product, LegalTrac. This product replaces the book version of *Index to Legal Periodicals*. Thomson (West) owns this product and only provides a limited number (10 percent) of full-text periodicals to be a part of this database.

The most recent licensed service that the library signed an agreement with is LLMC's Digital Library. This law library cooperative is providing their 100-million pages in Digital format through Internet access.

The library has the capability of tracking online usage to determine the usage patterns for these online resources. Adding these resources has been a major learning curve for the staff as well as the patrons. The staff has had a number of training sessions and will continue to be trained until they are comfortable using the products.

E-mail Service

Currently the Contra Costa County Department of Information Technology maintains the mail server for our library. All of the staff members have a county e-mail address, and a generic e-mail address was created with the name "infolib" to respond to questions from our Web site.

Internet Service

HalfPriceHosting is our current Internet service provider for our Web site and online library catalog. The staff updates the site through FTP changes to the provider. We changed our domain name from www.cccllib.com to www.cccpllib.org in May 2002. All of our library catalog and Web data files are now maintained by this vendor.

The CCCPLL Web site is continually upgraded with improved navigation. Our library assistant, who is the webmaster, is knowledgeable in the use of PhotoShop but still needs to be trained on the new programming techniques for Web pages such as Cascading Style Sheets (CSS) and JavaScript so that we can add consistency and interactivity to the Web site.

Training

An active training schedule has been presented to the staff, and they have been requested to participate. The LEXIS and Westlaw representatives have provided the staff with a number of group training sessions and some one-on-one assistance for some of the programs. Westlaw will no longer provide training to our patrons, due to a contract dispute, so the training will fall on the librarian.

The library has also utilized some of the Infopeople library training classes that have been offered at the Pleasant Hill Public Library's training center and online through the Internet. Limited library training is also provided through our membership in Baynet and the Golden Gateway Library Network. The county has voucher arrangements with Horizons (they previously used Comp USA) that should be considered as a resource. Relevant courses are also offered at Diablo Valley College that the staff can also attend.

The law librarian attends relevant conferences to increase her knowledge base through the seminars, meeting with vendors, and networking.

To capture the technology skills of the staff a high-level chart has been initiated. The chart is not complete and will require additional time and resources to list all of the technology skills that are required by the library staff as well as additional columns to list possible action items and time lines.

Sample Section from a Technology Plan / 63

Technology Skill Levels		
	Staff (ability ranges 1–5 with 5 high)	Comments
Technical Staff Skills		
PC skills		
Install and configure hardware	Level 3	Only one staff member is knowledgeable.
Load and update software	Level 3	Most software has been loaded by outside resources.
Troubleshoot and repair problems	Level 3	Most of the issues are located at the network level so most issues are hard to resolve.
LAN Skills		
Design network	Level 1	Rely on outside resource
Install and configure hardware	Level 1	Rely on outside resource
Load and update software	Level 1	Rely on outside resource
Troubleshoot and repair problems	Level 1	Rely on outside resource
Window Skills		
Understand basic file and folder organization	Level 2	
Web Browser Skills		
Research via browser	Level 4	Effective searchers
Applications		

Support

Currently the lack of onsite technical support is an issue. The staff are very resourceful and can fix copiers and provide minor assistance for the users when there are technology issues. The library does have the use of the county's technology help-desk for technological issues that are pertinent to their environment. The Contra Costa County Department of Information Technology (DOIT) will provide additional service but it would require a contract with predetermined hours at a rate of $100/hr. with an obligation for a minimum number of hours. Instead, arrangements have been made with an outside vendor to provide us with network support, updates, and desktop support. They have remote access to our server to effectively assist us and are also familiar with our library management vendor and our Web hosting source.

The library maintains its inventory on an active spreadsheet that is reviewed quarterly for accuracy. The inventory is grouped by the type of items, for example, hardware and software. It also provides pertinent information about those item such as date purchased, warranty coverage, and review dates for replacement.

Notes

1. Arthur Clarke. *The Lost Worlds of 2001.* 1972. From *Bartlett's Familiar Quotations,* 16th ed., Justin Kaplan, general editor (Boston: Little, Brown, 1992).
2. This section of a technology plan was prepared by Alice McKenzie.

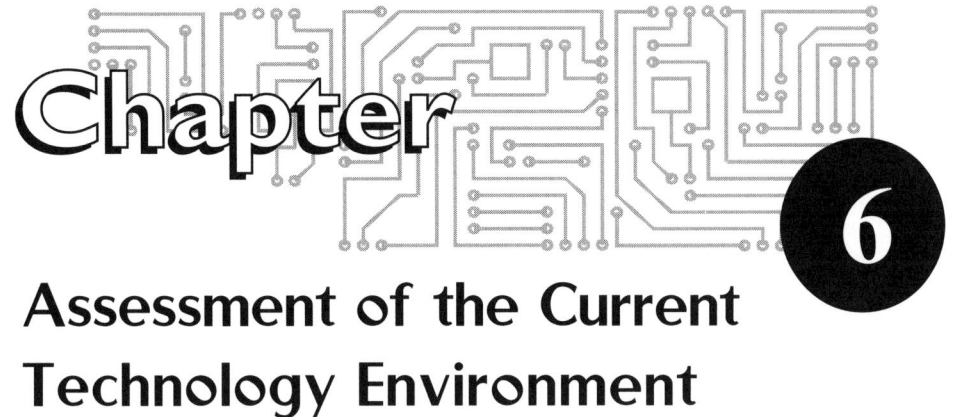

Chapter 6

Assessment of the Current Technology Environment

There is danger in reckless change; but greater danger in blind conservatism.—Henry George[1]

One of the constants of technology is that change is constant. And what worked yesterday may no longer work since one of the software components has been improved or upgraded and no longer works with other, often older, versions of companion software products. In addition, the needs of the library customers and staff members are also evolving. There may now be a demand to support wireless communication, audio and video streaming media, videoconferencing, downloading of very large documents and files, and so forth. This means that the technology plan must be assessed from a standard that is evolving and changing over time.

Is there a plan for an ongoing program for upgrading hardware and software and improving staff technology skills? It is possible to distinguish between a "normal" upgrade process of existing equipment, for example, desktop workstations and servers, computer operating systems, and additional disk space and computer memory to reflect the normal growth in files as the number of patrons increase. In addition, a library may need to upgrade equipment and software to reflect the introduction of a technology innovation or a new service. This latter upgrade should be addressed separately.

- **Physical facilities:** At times it is necessary to either add pieces of equipment or significantly expand the information technology components found within the library. Among the issues to be addressed are the following:

- Is there room within the existing conduits for additional data cables to be added?
- Are there sufficient power outlets to plug in the additional equipment at all of the planned locations?
- Will a specific electrical circuit become overloaded as additional devices are added? (Each device draws a minimum number of amps, and each electrical circuit is designed for a maximum number of amps, typically reflected in the size of the circuit breaker.)
- Are additional electrical circuits needed?
- Are additional data circuits needed?
- Are electrical outlets and data cable outlets located at some or all of the tables and other work areas that are provided for the library's customers?

- **Network infrastructure:** In general, networks are normally designed for peak, and not average, usage. When networks are designed for average use, they will not perform well in normal usage situations which, not surprisingly, have peaks and valleys of usage. Among the issues that should be addressed are the following:
  - There is an impact on the performance of a network as each additional workstation or other device is attached to a local area network. This "network overhead" should be recognized, and it may be necessary to reconfigure the LAN or increase the number of segments of the LAN.
  - Is the library thinking of adding "bandwidth intensive" applications such as listening to audio files or viewing video files to the desktop workstations for staff and the library's customers? If yes, then the bandwidth of the local area network may need to be increased.
  - What is the network typology? The basic typologies include hub and spoke (sometimes called a star), ring, and bus. The hub and spoke typology offers the greatest reliability since each device is connected to only one cable. All cables are then connected together at the hub (the actual device is a patch panel). A hub and spoke typology is typically used on one floor. (Libraries with multiple floors will typically have multiple hub and spoke cabling typologies, which are then connected together using a larger and faster backbone.) Ring and bus typologies reflect older approaches that are usually replaced with a hub and spoke typology.

Assessment of the Current Technology Environment / 67

- Is a wireless network currently implemented within the library? A wireless network will allow library customers with laptop computers and personal digital assistants or PDAs to gain access to the library's OPAC or Web site wherever the wireless network provides coverage.

- Some libraries have implemented a Bluetooth node so that people with Bluetooth-enabled devices can chat with one another.

- If the library has branches, then the issue of data communications between the branches and the library information system arises. Historically, most libraries have relied upon leased telephone lines such as a T1 line for this purpose. Other options include use of a frame relay service, microwave, or fiber optic link. Each of these options should be explored, since in a number of cases, the library can lower its annual operating costs. Note that not all options are available in all areas.

- Some libraries with branches have been adopting the use of Voice over IP or VOIP, which uses TCP/IP to provide voice communication between the branches and administrative headquarters in lieu of using the local telephone service.

- The library also needs a connection between the library and an Internet service provider (ISP) to provide access to the Internet for its customers and staff members. The service options in the library's locale should be periodically evaluated to determine if a better quality and more reliable service is available at a lower cost. In addition, more bandwidth may be required.

- **Network availability:** Issues such as reliability, response times, and sufficient bandwidth should be carefully examined. Obtaining network reliability and response time statistics can be informative in identifying if any bottlenecks may be occurring. Among the issues that might be examined are

    - The age and reliability of various network components,

    - The network typology,

    - The availability of trained staff to support and maintain the network, and

    - The speed of the network. Network interface cards (NICs) are used to connect each device to the network. In recent years, NICs have been manufactured so that they operate at either 10 Mbps or 100 Mbps—depending upon a switch setting. As libraries move beyond providing text access to providing access to audio and video files, then the basic speed of the network may need to be increased to 100 Mbps.

- **Computer hardware/operating system—servers:** To prepare an analysis in this area, it is necessary to determine the age (when was the server purchased?), the manufacturer, specific processor speed, amount of random access memory (RAM), and amount of disk space (and percent full) to assess whether the server should be upgraded or replaced. In general, upgrading a computer is not cost-effective—replacement should be done in most cases (processing power and system reliability increase, while costs decline over time).

  A number of servers may be installed for the library. Among these may be a file server, print server, e-mail server, domain controller, authenticator, library information system server, Internet filter, and fax server.

  - Today, most computer manufacturers will automatically provide a three-year warranty when a new server is purchased. You should determine the cost of maintenance for old servers and compare that with the cost of purchasing a new server with its lower maintenance costs.

  - If a server is used frequently, then having a fairly fast processor and sufficient RAM can improve the performance of the server.

  - Once disk space becomes more than 80 percent full, additional disk space must be provided.

  - The library should consider having a policy for the periodic replacement of all servers on a scheduled basis. In general, a library should plan for a server lasting between three to four years. Anything longer than five years means that the library is paying a fairly high amount of maintenance for service when compared to the cost of a new server (and a three-year warranty included in the price of the new server). Most computer manufacturers have a lease program so that at the end of the lease, the library can acquire a new server (and a new lease).

- **Computer hardware/operating system—desktops:** As with servers, to prepare an analysis for the desktop workstations it is necessary to determine the age (when was the server purchased?), the manufacturer, the specific processor speed, amount of RAM, and amount of disk space (and percent full) to determine whether the desktop computer should be upgraded or replaced. In general, upgrading a computer is not cost-effective—replacement should be done in most cases. The planned obsolescence of equipment and software is designed to maintain a steady course, not make way for innovation. Having a regular desktop computer replacement program helps to ensure that the library will experience relatively few operational problems. Typically, if RAM is less than 1 MB, then the desktop computer will operate at perceptibly lower speeds.

Some libraries, especially college and university libraries, will find that the information technology department of the college or university has assembled their computers. While this helps to lower initial costs, the library may find that as time goes on, getting these computers repaired or upgraded is difficult as finding spare parts and scheduling staff become problematic. Desktop computers have become a commodity item, and purchasing of these items from volume manufacturers such as Dell, HP, and IBM will make for fewer problems for the library.

The operating system for the server or desktop computer may be old and, in some cases, no longer supported by the manufacturer. This is especially true of Microsoft products, and libraries should recognize that the system reliability of the operating system improves with the more recent versions of Windows.[2] Does the library have licenses for all of the software on each desktop?

Does the library have a sufficient number of desktop workstations for staff and library patrons? (Is there a queue to use a desktop computer?) Is there space available (or could space be made available by rearranging some items or materials) for the planned additional desktop computers?

Should the library replace the existing "boxy" monitors with large, color flat-screen monitors? Flat-screen monitors use less desktop "real estate."

Does the library have a policy to replace a portion of the desktop workstations every three to four years? Since the reliability of the machines improves with time, replacement is generally less expensive than attempting to repair computers.

- **Software applications—library information system:** Almost all libraries have installed a library information system that has been licensed from a vendor. In addition to the purchase price for the license to install the software, the library pays an annual maintenance fee for software support and for the ability to load new releases of the software. Each new software release contains bug fixes and functional enhancements to one or more modules. Most vendors require a library to install a new software release within X number of months of its release. The vendor does not want to be in the position of attempting to support three or four or more versions of the software.

  Some library information system software will age well and continue to provide value for each library customer. Other software will become static and not respond to the needs of its customers. Thus, each library should consider replacing its library information system software every seven years or so. If a library is still using a character-based OPAC, then the library is a prime candidate for a new system.

Depending upon the size of the library, the software license for a new system can be fairly expensive. Thus, a library should consider creating an automated system replacement reserve fund. Some libraries budget for and set aside one-seventh of the cost of an automated library system each year. Then when it is time to select a new system, the library has the necessary funds to purchase a new system. This approach avoids the challenge of gaining approval and competing with other entities for the capital costs of the new system.

A library has access to four broad solutions for obtaining an automated library information system, including developing and maintaining a system in-house with library staff members, perhaps using open source software; an in-house system (sometimes called a turnkey system); sharing a system with several nearby libraries (a consortium or cooperative); or using a service known as an application service provider (ASP). These options are explored in greater detail in Appendix B.

- **Software applications—librarywide:** In addition to a library information system, some libraries provide additional software that some library employees use on a regular basis. Such software might be an accounting package, a human resources system, a payroll system, and so forth. Each package should be examined to determine its age, its annual maintenance costs, and its continuing value to the organization. Often other alternatives exist in the marketplace that should be considered, since these products may have functionality that is missing in the existing package, or costs may be reduced.

- **Software applications—desktops:** A majority of all libraries have installed office productivity software, for example MS Office, on all staff member desktop computers. Additional software packages that may be found on these machines include a Web browser, Adobe Acrobat, RealNetworks audio and video browser, an e-mail system, and more. Each of these software packages should be assessed to determine if it is compatible with the desktop operating system and so forth. While it is typically not important to have the "latest and greatest" release of each software package, it does make sense to ensure that an orderly upward migration path is planned, as support for older versions of these products is periodically suspended.

- **Technical support:**
  - *Patrons:* The problems encountered by library patrons are typically different, depending upon their location: within the library or remotely connected to the library. The library walks a fine line on the issue of technical support. As many library users are still of novice skill with computers, staff are often asked for basic assistance, which lies outside of the service the library wishes to offer. These conditions, as well as the infrequency of true technical support issues with these users, leads to most libraries providing assistance in a number of ways. Among these are informative handouts on a number of topics, for example, using an Internet browser; staff responding to specific questions that can be resolved quickly; and providing one-hour workshops or training sessions on various technology-related topics.

    In addition to helping patrons who request assistance while they are in the library, the library should provide a mechanism for remote users to report problems through the use of e-mail, chatting with a staff member online, and so forth. The library may wish to conduct a survey to determine the level of satisfaction that patrons are experiencing with the assistance and problem resolution services provided by the library.

  - *Library staff members:* The library information systems coordinator, the systems manager (or whatever the title), or their staff can routinely handle most computer issues. These problems can be reported by e-mail (for less time-sensitive issues) or by phone (for more serious issues).

    Some libraries have found that when everyday problems arise, having someone from each department who is well suited to handling routine problems and able to communicate and explain these issues with the remainder of the staff is an effective way to more quickly resolve problems and reduce the load on the library systems staff. Using frequent communication, staff can begin to understand why these problems do exist and what they can do to eliminate or to cope with them.

    Can the staff designated to support the library's information system and IT infrastructure

    - Determine the requirements to implement new technology?
    - Install and configure hardware?
    - Load and update software?
    - Troubleshoot and repair problems?

Is there a sufficient number of library systems staff to handle the volume of problems? If not, perhaps adding staff should be considered.

If another department provides support, for example the information technology department of the library's parent organization, are the quality and timeliness of service sufficient to meet the needs of the library? If not, then perhaps the library should suggest developing a service level agreement (SLA) that specifies the levels of service to be provided by the information technology department to the library. Often the fact that the library provides service beyond the normal office hours of 8:00 A.M. to 5:00 P.M. is not clearly recognized or appreciated by those providing support services.

- **Data—backups, virus protection:** Perhaps the most important physical asset of a library, aside from its collection, is the data the library has created that reflect its holdings (its catalog), as well as other important data files (patron files, circulation transaction files, serials files, and so forth). It would seem prudent to at least back up the data on a regular basis. In addition, hackers may also target the library's data files, and computer software programs directly or indirectly through the use of various viruses. Thus, among the issues that should be assessed are the following:

    - Are backups of data files performed on a regular basis? Most library information system vendors recommend that all files that have changed in the last 24 hours should be backed up each night (this can be scheduled and staff need not be present). All software programs and data files should be backed up each week (larger systems may back up all files more frequently).

    - Are the backup files or at least the full system backup files stored in an off-site location on a regular basis?

    - What safeguards are in place to guard against the introduction of viruses? Is a combination of hardware and antivirus software used (sometimes called a firewall)? Is the antivirus software updated on a frequent basis? Is antivirus software installed on each computer? How has the library fared in recent years in battling viruses and other forms of system abuse?

- **Staff skills:** In almost all libraries today, every staff member must be comfortable using information technology. Is there a regular training program that library staff members can sign up for? Are staff encouraged to attend technology-related classes offered at nearby colleges, universities, and commercial firms? Is there a technology-related staff development budget?

    Issues that should be addressed in assessing overall technology-based staff skills include the following:

- What level of technology-based skills do most staff members exhibit (poor, average, good, or very good) for these technologies?

    Operating system (Windows, Unix, and so forth)

    Web-browser skills (functions available when using a browser)

    Internet searching skills

    Commercial application software skills (e.g., MS Office)

    Library application specific skills

- Are technology-based workshops and classes offered on a regular basis within the library? Are workshops available for library staff within the larger organization?

- Is provision made within the library's budget for library staff members to attend classes hosted by commercial firms? Are staff encouraged to attend skill development courses offered before and after professional conferences?

- Do the periodic employee reviews of library staff members include a component assessing their technology competency?

- Are library staff members aware of, and do they follow, the library's computer use and Internet use policies?

A candid assessment of the skills of the staff members will assist the library in developing a framework for staff development and user education. Use of any technology implies a learning curve for any individual— whether a library staff member or library customer.

A sample section from a technology plan that assesses the library's current environment is presented next.

Sample Section from a Technology Plan

Assessment of Current Technology Environment[3]

To keep itself up-to-date with technology, the library has an ongoing plan for upgrading hardware and software and improving staff technological skills. While reviewing its technology inventory every three years, the library also arranges to assess its current technology environment. The assessment provides the library a clearer view of which portion of current technology requires improvement and which portion is worth maintaining to better serve the clientele.

The following section describes the assessment of the library's current technology environment. It indicates that the library's technology is fairly up-to-date and well prepared for technological changes in the future.

Network Infrastructure

Currently, the library does not have a plan for any major changes to its existing data network infrastructure. With its two existing T1 connections, the library still has plenty of bandwidth to use. If the public requires more bandwidth, reconfiguration will take place to move the staff's Internet traffic from the library's Internet T1 to the one that links to the city hall. In addition, if network security issues with wireless technology can be resolved, the library can also provide wireless Internet access to clients' laptops.

The library's wide area network (WAN) has been fairly stable and reliable. In the past four months, only two short outages have been reported. In addition, the network has an average response time of 10 to 16 milliseconds (ms). The response time between the city hall LAN and the library LAN is usually less than 10 ms.

The Library's fast-ethernet local area network (FELAN) of 100 Mbps is highly maintained and has been very stable and reliable as well. Although multimedia applications are ubiquitous these days, the library has never received requests for interactive videoconferencing and/or two-way video and audio streaming. Currently, only one-way streaming applications, such as Windows Media Player and Real Player, are available to the public and staff, and no significant network latency has been reported. Nonetheless, the library should still monitor closely its current bandwidth since the demand for multimedia streaming applications from clients is only a matter of time.

The cable modem provided by Adelphia will remain as a backup due to its bandwidth inconsistency. The current Cisco PIX 515 firewall will be reconfigured early next year to become the main traffic and security gatekeeper for the library's Internet. In addition, since expansion of the library's Teen Center and Computer/Homework Lab is anticipated, the library will purchase one additional Cisco 2600 switch/intelligent router for increasing traffic. Other than equipments for the Tech Center, the library will concentrate on replacing and upgrading existing equipment whenever feasible, instead of adding new physical hardware, due to space limitations and budget constraints. The maintenance of equipment such as routers and firewalls, and data connectivity, are mainly handled by contracts signed between the city and its equipment providers. The city renews the contracts on a regular basis. If the library were allowed to contact the vendors directly for trouble reporting, the library could enhance the quality of service by reducing the turnaround time for repair.

Although the library is fully wired with category-5 cabling, the addition of three new offices will require the library to either rewire or provide seamless extension on some portions of the cabling.

Computer Hardware/Operating System—Servers

The system specifications and usages of the library's servers are listed below.

Server	Hardware Specifications	Hard Drive Space Used	Special Software Installed	Current OS
LIBTAOS	• Intel Dual Pentium III 650 MHz • 2.0 GB RAM • 24 GB Hard Drive (SCSI)	• 18 GB (75%)	• Sirsi WorkFlows • Veritas (Backup Software) • Norton Antivirus v.7.6	• Microsoft NT4
LIBWEB2	• Intel Dual Pentium III 650 MHz • 392MB RAM • 8 GB Hard Drive (SCSI)	• 2.0 GB (25%)	• WebTrend • Norton Antivirus v.7.6	• Microsoft NT4
LIBMAIN	• Intel Pentium III 500 MHz • 655 MB RAM • 18 GB Hard Drive (SCSI)	• 4.0 GB (22%)	• Printer Server Software (APS) • Norton Antivirus v.7.6	• Microsoft NT4
LIBPROXY	• Intel Pentium III 1.3 GHz • 1.0 GB RAM • 31 GB Hard Drive (SCSI)	• 5.0 GB (16%)	• Surf Control v.4.2 • Norton Antivirus v.7.6	• Microsoft NT4
LIB-BDC	• Intel Pentium III 850 MHz • 256 MB RAM • 4.0 GB Hard Drive (SCSI)	• 1.8GB (45%)	• Norton Antivirus v.7.6	• Microsoft NT4

Based on the chart above, changes to the existing server farm are anticipated. First of all, given the fact that the automated system vendor will no longer provide support to its Windows NT4 platform, the library must seek a new operating system for its servers. At this point, the library is considering the Windows Server 2003 platform. According to Microsoft, the recommended system requirements for the enterprise edition of Windows Server 2003 are as follows:

- *CPU speed:* 733 MHz for Pentium systems
- *RAM:* 256 MB
- *Required disk space for setup:* 1.5 GB

It is prudent for the library to choose the Windows 2003 Server instead of the Windows 2000 Server platform because, according to Microsoft's product lifecycle table, it will retire its mainstream support for Windows 2000 Server on March 31, 2005. The retirement will affect all its customers, including ILS vendors, as it did with the Windows NT4 platform. However, based on the system requirements listed above, it is evident that, for the library to consider using the new Windows Server 2003 platform, it must either replace or upgrade its existing server hardware. Currently, only LIBPROXY and LIB-BDC servers have met the recommended system requirements for the Windows 2003 platform. Another criterion the library must consider is the compatibility of the existing server software with the new Windows Server 2003. So far, the installed software in each server takes about 640 MB of its disk space.

Second, the library will remove the LIBPROXY server permanently by reconfiguring the PIX firewall to handle traffic directing and filtering functions. In addition, it is confirmed that in fiscal year (FY) 2004–2005, the library will replace the LIBTAOS and LIBWEB2 servers with newer systems, preferably with Pentium 4 processors and with a minimum of 2 GB RAM each. The enhanced capabilities of these new servers will allow the library to engage in the purchase of digitized collections such as e-books.

The maintenance cost for the existing servers has been relatively low. All of the library's servers and desktops are purchased with manufacturers' standard three-year warranties, which cover both parts and labor. In addition, if a desktop is corrupted in such a way that it cannot be repaired without further investigation, a temporary unit will be provided.

The library is currently spending $17,000 a year on the ILS maintenance contract with the automated library system vendor. However, the library is aware of the vendor's inability to provide satisfactory support services and assistance. It does not have a standard 24-hour turnaround time for troubleshooting procedures, and its technical support staffs are not capable of assisting the library on issues beyond the product itself, such as system integration problems of its software with the library's network infrastructure. It seems that the vendor's technical support staff are only trained on their own products. As a result, the library is forced to resolve most of the technical issues with the vendor's products on its own.

Computer Hardware/Operating System—Desktops

Currently, a mixture of the Windows 2000 and Windows NT4 operating systems is installed on the public and staff desktops. All the new Dell systems, such as OptiPlex GX 240 and GX 260 models, come with the Windows 2000 platform, while the older systems such as Gateway, Compaq, and Dell OptiPlex GXa, GX1, GX1P, GX10, and GX 110 are still running on Windows NT4. In addition, the hard drives in most of the public desktops have relatively low usages; only 300 MB of each public desktop is used for software setup. The hard disk space usage is higher for the staff. The specifications for each of the desktop models are listed below in detail:

Brand and Model	Hardware Specifications	OS Installed
Compaq DeskPro P650	• Intel Pentium III 500 MHz • 128 MB RAM • 12 GB Hard Drive	Windows NT4
Dell OptiPlex GXa	• Intel Pentium II 333MHz • 128 MB RAM • 10GB Hard Drive	Windows NT4
Dell OptiPlex GX1	• Intel Pentium III 500 MHz • 128 MB RAM • 12-15GB Hard Drive	Windows NT4
Dell OptiPlex GX1P	• Intel Pentium III 500 MHz • 128 MB RAM • 15 GB Hard Drive	Windows NT4
Dell OptiPlex GX110	• Intel Pentium III 500 MHz • 128 MB RAM • 15 GB Hard Drive	Windows NT4
Dell OptiPlex GX 240	• Intel Pentium 4 1.5GHz • 256 MB RAM • 30 GB Hard Drive	Windows 2000 Professional
Dell OptiPlex GX 260	• Intel Pentium 4 2.4GHz • 256 MB RAM • 30 GB Hard Drive	Window 2000 Professional
Gateway E-4200	• Intel Pentium III 450 MHz • 128 MB RAM • 12 GB Hard Drive	Windows NT 4

While the Windows Professional 2000 platform may have seemed to be a good candidate to replace Windows NT4, Microsoft, in fact, is also phasing out the Windows 2000 platform. According to Microsoft's product lifecycle table, the mainstream supports to the Windows 2000 Professional platform will be retired on March 31, 2005, while its Office 2000 Professional suite mainstream support will be retired on June 30, 2004. Considering the supporting time frame from Microsoft for the above products, the library should choose to run its desktops with the Windows XP Professional platform to avoid planning another costly upgrade or replacement of software and hardware in the near future. However, this means the library will have to replace the majority of its current desktops due to higher system requirements for Windows XP Professional. The recommended system requirements for Windows XP Professional are as follows:

- *Computer/processor:* 300 MHz or higher Pentium-compatible CPU.
- *Memory*: At least 128 megabytes (MB) of RAM or higher; more memory generally improves responsiveness.
- *Hard disk space for setup:* 1.5 GB free space.
- *Other peripherals:* CD-ROM or DVD drive

Although it may seem that the library's hardware specifications for the desktops meet the minimum system requirements for Windows XP, to ensure functionality and performance of the systems, the library should really seek higher standards for its systems.

In addition, the library will purchase 14 new public desktops, 4 staff desktops, and 1 public print server for the expansion of the Teen Center and Computer/Homework Lab once the project commences.

Software Applications—Library Information System

The library currently uses the Z39.50 standard protocol for communication with other libraries for information retrieval and uses TCP/IP for communication protocol. File Transfer Protocol (FTP), although not available to all the staff or the public, is still a powerful protocol used by the Information Technology Services Department for the library's software upgrade downloads. The library uses Simple Mail Transfer Protocol (SMTP) as the main e-mail protocol standard. Although these protocol standards are not likely to change, the library should be aware of various new releases in protocol versions. In addition, since the choice of operating system may affect the level of difficulty during the Z39.50 server installation and configuration, the library should explore the configuration instruction of the new operating systems thoroughly prior to each installation.

Finally, since XML is gradually replacing XHTML and HTML coding for Web pages, many electronic database vendors as well as the Library of Congress are incorporating the code in their databases and Web designs. To ensure interoperability and enhance manageability, the library should begin exploring and incorporating XML for its databases and Web site.

Software Applications—Librarywide

The library is anticipating at least one major and one minor upgrade release from the automated library system vendor once a year for its integrated library system (ILS). Major upgrades are scheduled after hours, while minor updates are completed during the off-peak hours of the library.

The library should also work on providing seamless access to the subscribed electronic databases through its existing OPAC interface. Clients would not have to enter their identification numbers multiple times after logging into the library's OPAC.

Software Applications—Desktops

Since the majority of the desktops in the library use Microsoft software, update and upgrade processes are performed frequently. In addition, the library is also following Microsoft's changes in service availability since Microsoft is a de facto standard, and any changes on its part usually affect other software vendors immediately. Although a change to the library's desktops' operating systems is expected, the library is seeking to continue using existing Microsoft software such as Office 2000, Project, Outlook, and so forth. However, as mentioned earlier, Microsoft plans to retire its mainstream support to the majority of its Microsoft 2000 products by 2005. Moreover, in general, Microsoft offers a minimum of five years of mainstream support from the date a product becomes available. Customers have the option to purchase two-year extended support at the end of mainstream support. In addition, online self-help support is available to its customers for at least eight years.

The following description of Microsoft's mainstream, extended, and online self-help support services is extracted directly from the official Microsoft site:[4]

Support Type	Description
Mainstream Support	Includes all the support options and programs, such as no-charge incident support, paid incident support, support charged on an hourly basis, support for warranty claims, and hotfix support.
Extended Support	Includes all paid support options, as well as security-related hotfix support, which is provided at no charge. Non-security related hotfix support requires a separate Extended Hotfix Support Contract to be purchased within 90 days after Mainstream support ends. Microsoft will not accept requests for warranty support, design changes, or new features during the Extended support phase.
Self-Help Online Support	By using Microsoft's online Knowledge Base articles, Frequently Asked Questions (FAQs), troubleshooting tools, and other resources, customers can quickly resolve their issues without contacting Microsoft directly.

The following chart lists the product support time line from Microsoft's "Product Lifecycle Table" for software currently used in the library. By keeping track of these support retirement dates, the library would be able to plan ahead any upgrade or installation of software applications for its desktops and servers.

Microsoft Product	General Availability Date	Mainstream Support Retired Date	Extended Retired Support Date
Windows NT4 Server	7/29/1996	12/31/2002	12/31/2004
Windows NT4 Workstation	7/29/1996	6/30/2002	12/31/2004
Windows 2000 Professional	3/31/2000	3/31/2005	3/31/2007
Windows XP Professional	12/31/2001	12/31/2006	12/31/2008
Office 2000 Professional (includes PowerPoint, Excel, Word, Access, and Outlook)	6/27/1999	6/30/2004	6/30/3006
Office XP Professional (includes PowerPoint, Excel, Word, Access, Outlook, and FrontPage)	5/31/2001	6/30/2006	6/30/2008
Project 2000	5/28/1999	6/30/2004	N/A
Publisher 2000	9/7/1999	6/30/2004	N/A

Once the expansion of the Teen Center and Computer/Homework Lab has been confirmed, an additional 15 to 18 software licenses must be purchased for the new systems that will be added to the expanded facility and the new employees' systems. The software licenses include programs like Microsoft Windows, Office, and so forth.

Last, since the library is seeking to provide a public desktop designated for disabled patrons equipped with voice recognition technology, it should start exploring the product market and various options. The library will consider installing this software by reconfiguring one of the existing stations before it decides to purchase a new one. The voice recognition station will be situated along with other assistive-adaptive devices in one of the library's study rooms.

Technical Support

- **Users:** While immediate technical support is available, the technical staffs and system administrator in the library are part-time employees. Therefore, the library should standardize its trouble reporting procedures to include available hours so clients would not have to run around the library looking for technical assistance. In addition, a standard troubleshooting procedure should be established and provided to all technical support aides so they can quickly go over the list to note things they have already checked before contacting the system administrator. This can reduce the turnaround time by not repeating the troubleshooting procedures already completed by the aides.

- **Network:** As noted previously, the library does not have maintenance contracts with data services and equipment providers directly. If there is a network problem related to its reliability, response times, and bandwidth, the library must report it to the city's senior network administrator, who will then contact the service or equipment provider for troubleshooting if he or she is unable to resolve the problem. While the usual turnaround time with some of the providers is four or more hours, such trouble reporting procedures can further lengthen the turnaround time, especially if problems happen in the library after the city's business hours. Since the library has its own information system service section, it should consider asking the city for permission to contact the service and equipment providers directly if the equipment and connection are located in the library's information system service office.

- **Data:** Although the library gives high priority to data backup and protection, continuous renewal and update of antivirus detection and backup software programs must be performed in a timely manner to ensure full and complete protection at all times.

Staff Skills

Currently, the library is providing application trainings only on an as-needed basis. The library's system administrator is sent to various intensive technical training or covered by special training budgets.

The library must seek to provide more technical training for its staff members. It must be able to motivate staff to take these training courses by providing both budget and time. For example, the library should consider offering classes on a regular basis to provide more in-depth training on library applications, the structure of the Internet and protocols such as TCP/IP, FTP, and SMTP, and basic maintenance of workstations and LANs.

The library should also establish benchmark-training guidelines for major staff positions to ensure that all the staff members receive adequate technical training for their responsibilities. If possible, the library should also include training issues as part of every staff member's annual work plan.

To ensure that the library stays current with technology, assessment of this kind must be done on a regular basis. The assessment allows the library to acknowledge the strengths and weaknesses of its current technology environment and provides a clear guideline for the library to budget its technology expenses.

Notes

1. Henry George. *Social Problems*. From *Bartlett's Familiar Quotations,* 16th ed., Justin Kaplan, general editor (Boston: Little, Brown, 1992).
2. See for example, http://www.microsoft.com/windows2000/support/lifecycle/.
3. This section of a technology plan was prepared by Vivienne Khan.
4. *Microsoft Support Lifecycle*. 2003. Available at: : http://support.microsoft.com/default.aspx?scid=fh%3Ben-us%3Blifecycle&LN=EN-US&x=14&y=11 (accessed October 12, 2003); *System Requirements* [Windows Server 2003 System Requirements]. 2003. Available at: http://www.microsoft.com/windowsserver2003/evaluation/sysreqs/default.mspx (accessed October 10, 2003); *Windows 2000 System Requirements.* 2003. Available at: http://www.microsoft.com/windows2000/professional/evaluation/sysreqs/default.asp (accessed October 10, 2003).

Evaluation of a Library's Web Site

> *Far too little thought has been given to how technology is being permitted to change libraries.*—Stanley M. Katz[1]

First impressions clearly are very important. Yet even a good first impression will not keep users coming back to a library's Web site time after time. As libraries have developed their own Web pages, it is quite clear that usability normally takes a back seat to other system factors, for example, providing links to lots of information. When a library's Web page has not undergone any fundamental change for three months, six months, a year, or more, it is sending a clear message to those who take the time to visit—the library does not care![2] Web sites that are "sticky" are sites that provide the user with compelling reasons to return again and again. The reasons for the "stickiness" might be current information resources, ease of use, or other related factors.

Too often the realities of Moore's Law, which states, "An information retrieval system will tend not to be used whenever it is more painful and troublesome for a customer to have information than for him not to have it," are ignored.[3]

In some libraries, the number of people visiting the library and asking reference questions has dropped, often significantly during the last half of the 1990s. Where are people going to get their information? The Web! Surprise, surprise! Nearly three-quarters (73 percent) of college students say they use the Internet more than the library, while only 9 percent say they use the library more than the Internet for information searching.[4]

Web Site Design

Web sites are designed to provide access to a plethora of information. Unfortunately, library Web sites don't employee electronic shopping carts, so we are unable to determine how many Web site visitors become frustrated and abandon the site never to return again. However, a library must begin to employ software analysis tools to determine at what point users are abandoning a Web site. Armed with this information, changes can be made to the site.

The experience of using a Web site is tied to a variety of factors, including how the site is organized and what navigation features, such as buttons, tabs, menus, links, graphics, a site map, and a search engine. are provided. Users come with a set of expectations when they are visiting a Web site, and to be successful, the Web site must meet or exceed these expectations.

An ideal library Web site will offer access to the library's OPAC, electronic information resources, and interactive reference services 24 hours a day, 7 days a week . The Web site will provide basic information about the library, including its location, hours, upcoming events, and so forth. Increasingly, it will also provide access to other community-based resources.[5] The importance of the library's Web site cannot be overstated. The Web site is the window through which library customers can view the wide array of accessible information resources without actually physically visiting the library. And for some libraries, remote access to the library is the way one-fourth or more of the library's customers obtain library services. Perhaps a library should compare the percent of the budget devoted to the library's Web site to providing services in the physical buildings.

A library's Web site may be in one of three evolutionary stages:

- **We are here:** This is a task-oriented, traditional library message. In a similar vein, early commercial Web sites were often called "brochure ware" sites.

- **User-centered digital library:** In addition to having access to the library's online catalog and several online databases, users are able to find out information about the status of various activities and communicate with the library to place a hold, change their mailing address, and so forth.

- **Personalization:** Users are able to specify how they want "their" version of the library's Web site, including the OPAC, to look and feel. Some library Web sites are employing XML-based services to provide up-to-the-minute news and other information of interest to a library customer. Others are providing links to blogs that may be of interest. Short for **Web log**, a blog is a Web page that serves as a publicly accessible personal journal that is typically updated daily.

Before addressing some of the fundamental design concepts that should be followed when creating or redesigning a Web site, it is important to know the answers to the following questions:

- **Why has the library created a Web site?** What is the purpose of the site? What specific groups of people are expected to use the Web site?

- **What does the library want to accomplish with this site?** Will the site provide more than simple information about the library and access to the library's Web OPAC?

- **What does the library want users to accomplish with this site?** What can the library patrons accomplish directly? Can they customize the site? Can they sign up for an alert service (selective dissemination of information)?

- **What will keep a user on your site?** Does your site provide access to subject pathfinders with links to recommended Web sites? Can the library patron interact directly with a reference librarian using e-mail, instant messaging, or chat? Is the library adding content-rich information resources on an ongoing basis?

- **What will encourage a user to return?** Is content updated regularly? Does the library provide free e-mail, downloadable wallpaper, e-postcards, community message boards, and so forth?

A number of usability experts suggest that Web site design involves a number of characteristics that must be present so that visitors will find the Web site compelling and return again and again. These characteristics include the following:

1. **Graphic design neither helps nor hurts**. Larger graphics will, however, slow the download time of a Web page and for that reason alone are discouraged.

2. **Text links are vital**. Users don't want to read; they skip explanatory text and move directly to links.

3. **Navigation and content are inseparable**. Users have no patience, so the visitor should have a clear sense of how to accomplish a variety of tasks at the Web site.

4. **Information retrieval is different than surfing**. Thus, a Web site search engine is almost a mandatory requirement. Users don't want to scroll through long lists to find information of value.

5. **Web sites aren't like software**. People are often forced to use bad software, but another Web site is only a click away. What works well in a Windows environment may not work well using the Web, since the underlying technologies and the user interface are different.

A number of usability experts recommend that high quality Web sites should:

- **Provide locally developed information**. Visitors to a Web site are seeking information that will be of value. This is particularly true and hopefully obvious when people visit a library's Web site. If the library's Web site supports important tasks or offers useful services that support a user (for example, e-mail to a librarian, the ability to check on the status of reserve materials), users are more likely to return to the site when confronted with the task of locating information resources.

- **Be easy to find and access**. The use of tabs has become increasingly prevalent in Web sites since tabs indicate to the user what options are available. Tabs provide obvious navigation assistance. The tabs suggest a physical space, and what is behind the tab is obvious (assuming the tab label is clear). Tabs are, however, only one of several techniques to make navigation within a Web site intuitive.

- **Be well formatted and edited**. Consistency of design assists the user in navigation. The library should consider developing, and then frequently updating, a style guide that clearly delineates the look and feel of the library's Web site.[6] Recognize that both novice and experienced individuals will use the Web site and that both groups should be able to navigate smoothly.

    Hypertext links that are no longer up to date or that point to resources that no longer exist are an obvious source of frustration for users of the library's Web site. The experience of a number of search engines is that about 25 percent of all links more than a year old will no longer work. This condition is sometimes referred to as "linkrot." Developers and designers of Web pages should use a software tool to check the integrity of all links on a regular basis and repair any links as quickly as possible. One of the reasons for linkrot is that some Web sites are constantly evolving, which means that the site is pointing to pages that change continuously.[7]

- **Recognize that people are trying to find something of value**. Recent research found that almost 75 percent of users were searching for multiple pieces of information, while another 25 percent were looking for something specific.[8] In addition, users are visiting a Web site to compare or choose something to make a decision. Second, they want to acquire a fact or a document, and third, users want to gain an understanding of some topic. Thus, the site needs to be well structured and organized. According to Jared Spool, information has a "scent" that people pick up on as they move from page to page (Peter Pirolli at Xerox PARC calls information scent "information foraging").[9] And Marcia Bates has described the approaches that people take to find information of value, all of which can be supported in the Web environment, as "berrypicking."[10] Thus, strive for efficiency. Make the paths to an information resource as short and productive as possible.

- **Be predictable**. A consistent look and feel, consistent terminology, and avoidance of jargon (both library and technology buzz words) will improve the overall usability of the Web site. Assist users in deciding where not to go through the use of clear navigation signposts. Make sure that your site uses existing Web conventions (for example, use blue underline for hyperlinks, no underline for normal text). Make sure the paths from one point to another are as direct as possible (eliminate unnecessary clicks). Should users become lost, they are not likely to return!

- **People choose to search or browse**. At some sites, almost half of all users will use the Web site's search engine.[11] The success of searching a specific Web site is not known, but the success rate in searching for a broader set of information available via the Web is truly disappointing—between 60 and 80 percent of people fail.[12]

- **When browsing, people will use a hierarchy**. Web sites that have many layers (depth) should provide guidance using coordinated colors, graphics, tabs, or navigation bars. Consistency in the design and rendering of navigation bars on each page, regardless of level, is an important concept to consider. Color is particularly effective to differentiate different types of information and for setting the tone of a Web site. Design in black and white and then add one or two colors.

- **Each Web page should stand on its own**. Limiting each Web page to one concept or idea allows the user to quickly scan the page and decide to select something or move on.

- **Speed is an important factor,** since most users won't wait more than 10 seconds to download a Web page (or the alternative definition for WWW becomes "World Wide Wait").[13] There are a number of Web site performance testing software tools that will indicate where bottlenecks are occurring.[14] Don't use big, slow graphics—no matter how impressive you think they are.

Usability Guidelines

While a number, perhaps a majority, of authors considered to be usability experts have developed usability guidelines, these seem to be based on observations and personal recommendations rather than the results of careful research.[15] The majority of these guidelines could be placed into three broad groups: navigational characteristics, practical considerations, and visual characteristics.

Roger Black suggests that good Web sites come from the principles that have informed quality print design for hundreds of years. His 10 rules of good design include the following:

1. Put content on every page. And make it easy to read since people skim and surf a Web page.
2. The first color is white.
3. The second color is black.
4. The third color is red or . . .
5. Never letter space lowercase.
6. Never set a lot of text type in all caps.
7. A cover should be a poster.
8. Use only one or two typefaces.
9. Make everything as big as possible. Use font with larger point sizes.
10. Get lumpy! Break up the consistent look and feel occasionally.[16]

Nancy Everhart, of St. Johns University, has developed a framework to evaluate external Web sites that a library could use in making a determination to catalog a Web site or to provide a link to that Web site on the library's own Web site. The individual making the evaluation first distributes a total of 100 points to nine evaluation factors (this allows a library to place more emphasis on currency, content/information, or authority and less emphasis on multimedia, for example). Sites that meet some minimum acceptable score, for example, 60 out of the possible 100, could then be considered candidates that would be of value to a library and its users. The evaluation factors include:

- **Currency:** The Web site tells visitors when the information was last updated, who is responsible for the accuracy of the information, and whom to contact for a variety of purposes, for example, reference, circulation, webmaster, and so forth.

- **Content/information:** The content itself should dictate the design of a Web site without introducing distracting features or "cool" technologies. Is the information accurate? If a document is provided, is the source of the document apparent? Are there any disclaimers, or should there be? The value of hypertext is that it is possible to break apart content into smaller pieces. For a library Web site, the library may want to provide access to the library's own online catalog, commercial indexes and databases, and Internet resources as well as local resources.

- **Authority:** Users of a library's Web site are expecting that the same techniques used by librarians in selecting quality resources to add to the physical collection will also be applied to resources that are made available via the Web.

- **Navigation:** A uniform look and feel will assist the user in avoiding a chaotic presentation. The library's Web site and OPAC must be visually appealing. Consistent use of color, page layout, and other design elements can be used to present Web pages that are of value to the user. The navigational tools that are selected should be able to accommodate first-time users as well as the more experienced searcher. Users should always know where they are in a Web site (color-coded pages, graphics, a navigation bar, and a site map have been used effectively at some sites). Multiple navigation styles should be supported, including searching, browsing, effective use of links, graphic links, an FAQ list, and so forth. Between 35 and 50 percent of site visitors use the search feature for navigation purposes.[17]

- **Experience:** The overall experience of using a Web site must be straightforward and intuitive. One of the hallmarks of an intuitive site is that it is organized logically and that it supports a wide array of users and technology.

- **Multimedia:** If your Web site has links to or uses multimedia tools, for example, Adobe's PDF files, Shockwave's Flash, RealAudio, RealVideo, PowerPoint, and so forth, the Web site should alert the user of the need to have a plug-in software module installed (and provide a direct link to Web sites that allow the downloading of the tool without distractions).

- **Treatment:** Does the site achieve its purpose of providing access to information about a particular topic? Are there valuable links to Web sites that provide complementary information?

- **Access:** The ways in which visitors to the library's Web site are seeking information can be conveniently divided into two groups (similar to online catalog users): those that are *searching* for specific information and those that want to *browse* on a topic. Ensuring that both of these approaches are easy will mean that users will be able to locate what they are interested in. If they cannot, then they will become exasperated, leave, and likely never return again.

- **Miscellaneous:** Speed of the Web page downloads time. Other factors that might be important would be added here. Some Web sites load so slowly that the Web has been called the "World Wide Wait."

As library Web sites have grown in size and complexity, attempting to maintain an HTML-only site will display the limitations of this tool. A design approach that uses an application server with a database of information resources will allow the library's Web site to scale. While HTML is great for displaying data, a database is a good way to manage data about information resources. A database-driven Web site will combine the best of both worlds and reduce the personnel costs associated with maintaining a Web site.[18] Libraries should embed keyword attributes in a HTML META tag in their Web sites and HTML documents, since this significantly improves accessibility when a search engine is used.[19]

Other checklists have been developed that may also be useful. The Nielsen evaluation criterion takes into account features and stylistic applications that have been widely accepted as informal Web standards.[20]

In addition, the Web Accessibility Initiative of the W3C developed the *Web Content Accessibility Guidelines 1.0*.[21] These 66 guidelines provide recommendations on how Web content can be made more accessible to individuals with disabilities.

Evaluating Your Library's Web Site

This section of the technology plan should present a description of the library Web site (its address, use, and use of standards in creating the site) and its usability (you may want to compare it to two or three other similar Web sites). Select the evaluation criteria based on a literature review, conduct the evaluation, and document your results and recommendations.

Remember that some (most) of the readers of your plan may not be familiar with the library's Web site, so including a screen shot is a good idea. If possible you should indicate the amount of Web site traffic—the number of hits and other statistical information, if it is available.

Sample Section from a Technology Plan

Introduction[22]

This section of the technology plan evaluates the San Francisco Public Library's Web site. It reviews some of the literature regarding evaluation criteria and provides an evaluation and analysis of SFPL's Web site based on this literature. Specifically, the literature retrieved and reviewed provides the guidelines to SFPL's Web site use, use of standards, and usability.

The World Wide Web has a lot of information resources at the fingertips for the masses. Unfortunately a lot of information on the Web may not be valid or current. This is why library Web sites are important, because a library Web site is going to provide information from a source that is usually noted as being valid and current. Librarians should evaluate Internet information resources to determine the quality or appropriateness of information for users. Furthermore, a library's Web interface is a crucial point in the success and satisfaction of librarians and patrons. Susan McMullen has noted that "as libraries move forward into the digital age, the Web becomes increasingly important for meeting the needs of all users. A library Web interface represents an important meeting ground between the information professional and the individual who is seeking information."[23]

In terms of service, the library Web site should offer the patron access to the library's OPAC and to electronic resources. An exceptional library Web site should also provide information about the library, location of service outlets, hours of all service outlets, upcoming programs, services provided, etc. The Web interface should be clear and uncluttered, easy to maneuver, and provide different access levels to accommodate different learning styles.

Evaluation of SFPL's Web Site and Comparison to San Jose Library

To begin evaluating SFPL's Web site we can use a worksheet developed by Dr. Nancy Everhart, of St. John's University, Division of Library and Information Science.[24] This evaluation will compare SFPL to the San Jose Library (SJL), which can assist in providing better answers in evaluating the results such as a need for changes or improvements. Both Bay area libraries utilize the same automation vendor, Innovative Interfaces.

Everhart applies nine evaluation factors and applies points to each factor:

- Currency (0 to 10 Points)
- Content/information (0 to 10 Points)
- Authority (0 to 10 Points)
- Navigation (0 to 10 Points)
- Experience (0 to 10 Points)
- Multimedia (0 to 10 Points)
- Treatment (0 to 10 Points)
- Access (0 to 10 Points)
- Miscellaneous (0 to 10 Points)

Figure 7.1 is a visual example of how SFPL's Web site is presented to the user.

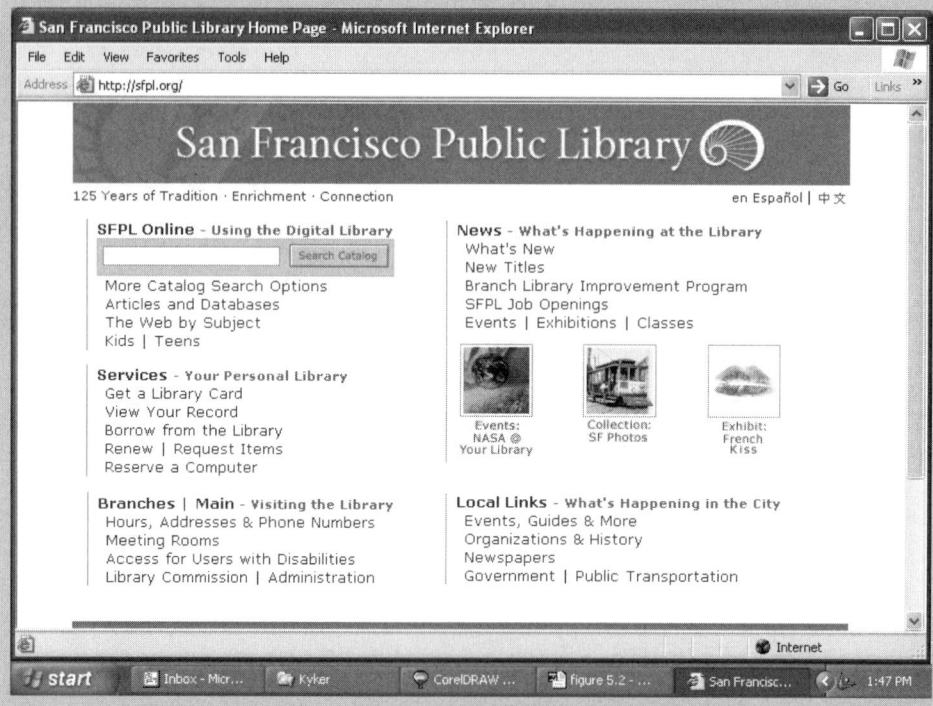

Figure 7.1. San Francisco Public Library Web Site

The following chart lists the scores for SFPL's evaluation, and the reasons for the scores.

Factor	Evaluation	Score
Currency	• Most of the information has been updated in the last month.	10
Content/information	• SFPL provides access to all of the following: library information, library OPAC, commercial indexes, Internet resources, and local links.	10
Authority	• SFPL provides links to Web resources and provides contact information via e-mail.	10
Navigation	• The links are easy to identify and grouped logically. Easy to navigate.	10
Experience	• The experience fulfills its intended purpose for the most part, and no broken hypertext links are present.	9

Sample Section from a Technology Plan / 93

Factor	Evaluation	Score
Multimedia	• No sounds or video enhance the site. except for some graphics. • No plug-ins are present.	5
Treatment	• Provides links to other library Web sites.	10
Access	• SFPL provides a Web site search and a library OPAC search.	10
Miscellaneous	• SFPL's Web page downloaded in one second.	10
Total		84

In comparison, figure 7.2 is a visual of how SJL's Web site is presented to the user.

Figure 7.2. San Jose Library Web Site

The following chart presents the scores for SJL's evaluation and the reasons for the scores.

Factor	Evaluation	Score
Currency	• Most of the information has been updated in the last two months.	7
Content/information	• SJL provides access to all of the following—library information, library OPAC, commercial indexes, and Internet resources—but no local links.	7
Authority	• SJL provides links to Web resources and provides contact information via e-mail.	10
Navigation	• Ease of navigation is good; could use a little work on organizing headings.	8
Experience	• The experience fulfills its intended purpose for the most part, and no broken hypertext links are present.	9
Multimedia	• No sounds or video enhance the site, except for some graphics. • No plug-ins are present.	5
Treatment	• Provides links to other library Web sites.	10
Access	• SJL provides a Web site search and a library OPAC search.	10
Miscellaneous	• SJL's Web page downloaded in nine seconds.	7
Total		73

SFPL has a score considered in the good range for its Web site, whereas SJL's score is considered average. In comparison, three factors that stand out between the two sites are currency, access to local links, and download time. These three factors alone attributed to a better score for SFPL. I would surmise that SJL's combined efforts of a public and academic library might contribute to some of these factors. For example, local links may not be as relevant for students, which may be the reason for a lack of this feature. Also, conflicts between the two divisions (public versus academic) may be hindering the quality of the site; more emphasis might be placed on academic services and not public.

Things That Work Well for SFPL's Web Site

When combining a usability study conducted in 2002 by Alison J. Head & Associates[25] and John Kupersmith's[26] article "Library Terms That Users Understand," we can see that SFPL has indeed initiated several factors to provide ease of use for users of it Web site. These factors are as follows:

- Indentation of the blue subcategories listings helps make these subcategories more usable.
- Small images in the boxes are utilized, and there are no large graphics or images to download.
- The layout is done extremely well, very usable for users.
- "Target words," such as *New Books, Kids,* and *Teens* are used.
- SFPL emphasizes alternatives to the catalog by prominently placing links such as *Articles and More* and *The Web by Subject.*
- SFPL provides intermediate pages in cases where a top-level menu choice presents ambiguities that can't be resolved in the search query. An example of this is *Advance Search,* which leads to a page offering journal article databases, news databases, etc.

Moreover, SFPL's Web site also conforms to W3C recommendations and other standards, as evidenced by the W3C icon on the bottom of its home page. W3C checks HTML documents for conformance to W3C HTML and XHTML recommendations and other HTML standards. SFPL's Web site was checked and found to use valid XHTML 1.0 Transitional.

Recommendations

On the other hand, SFPL can increase its usability by adhering to the recommendations mentioned in the some of the usability studies discussed in current literature. Defining key labels for specific available resources is not always inherent to a user. Library jargon can plague the user's ability to search for the availability of resources. However, SFPL does a decent job avoiding library jargon. Specific recommendations to increase the usability of SFPL's Web site include the following:

- Increase the font size of the subcategory links for better readability from smaller monitors.
- Darken or brighten the color of the subcategory links to create more contrast.
- Change "administration" to "Policies and Procedures." Some users may be unclear that this is a link to policies and procedures and library reports.

- Change the subcategory link "Access for Users" under Library Locations to Services.

- Provide a more prominent link to the Q&A café from the first screen. Change the link from the bottom of the screen and provide a link under "SFPL Online" or "Services."

- Provide a glossary of library terms.

- Provide Z39.50 access to other library catalogs.

- Incorporate the sharing of subscription resources.

- Continuously expand community information files.

- Provide links to Internet/intranet resources offered by other San Francisco city departments.

- Encourage the establishment of links from other local organizations to the library's Web site.

Aside from the actual Web site, SFPL also can improve access to its information infrastructure and to technology by adhering to its 2003–2006 Strategic Plan as approved by the San Francisco Public Library Commission on October 2, 2003. These plans are as follows:

- Install wireless capabilities in library facilities so users may use SFPL's services with their own computing devices, in addition to providing plug-in access.

- Continue to develop and expand library services electronically. This would include online services such as library forms (library card applications and comment forms) so that services provided within SFPL facilities are also available to online users.

- Ensure that SFPL's technological infrastructure and systems support the development of an online learning environment in a variety of subject areas and incorporate a high quality of learning aids such as online tutorials, pathfinders, webcasts, and Web links to tutorials in a variety of subjects that will facilitate user access and learning.

- Train staff in instruction techniques and subject-specific topics and provide the technological infrastructure to help staff provide appropriate classes and one-on-one guidance to users.

Summary

In general the information available and the power of SFPL's site is unrecognized and therefore the site is underutilized. I would surmise that this is true for many library sites. As stated by McMullen, usability testing is an eye-opening experience for many libraries. Without user input, libraries may be tempted

> to design from their own perspective and using the jargon of the profession. Understanding how users interpret our links and interact with library Web sites is important for a usable interface.

Notes

1. Stanley M. Katz. Information Technology: Don't Mistake a Tool for a Goal. *The Chronicle of Higher Education*, June 15, 2001, B7.

2. Helge Clausen. Evaluation of Library Web Sites: The Danish Case. *The Electronic Library*, 17 (2), April 1999, 83–87; L. A. Clyde. The Library as Information Provider: The Home Page. *The Electronic Library*, 14 (6), 1996, 549–58; Randy Rice. *Randy Rice's Software Testing Page: Web Usability Checklist*. Available at: http:www.riceconsulting.com/webusability.htm (accessed August 1, 2004); E. B. Lily and C. Van Fleet. Measuring the Accessibility of Public Library Home Pages. *Reference and User Services Quarterly*, 40 (2), Winter 2000, 176–80.

3. C. N. Mooers. Mooers's Law: Or Why Some Retrieval Systems are Used and Others Are Not. *American Documentation*, 11 (3), 1990, 1.

4. Steve Jones. *The Internet Goes to College: How Students Are Living in the Future with Today's Technology*. Washington, DC: Pew Internet & American Life Project, September 15, 2002.

5. K. Diaz. The Role of the Library Web Site. *Reference and User Services Quarterly*, 38 (1), Fall 1998, 41–48.

6. Patrick J. Lynch and Sarah Horton. *Web Style Guide: Basic Design Principles for Creating Web Sites*. New Haven, CT: Yale University Press, 1999. Also, examples of Web style guides can be found at http://www.ber.org/stylemanual/, http://www.beadsland.com/weapas/, http://webreference.com/html/, and http://www.sun.com/styleguide/.

7. Link-checking programs include WWW Link Checker (for Unix systems), http://www.ugrad.cs.ubc.ca/spider/q7f192/branch/checker.html: lvrfy: A HTML Link Verifier, http://www.cs.dartmouth.edu/~crow/lvrfy.html; and MOMspider (Multi-Owner Maintenance spider), http://www.ics.uci.edu/WebSoft/MOMspider/WWW94/paper.html.

8. Jakob Nielsen. The 3Cs of Critical Web Use: Collect, Compare, Choose. *Alertbox*, April 15, 2001. Available at: http://www.useit.comalertbox/20010415.html (accessed August 1, 2004).

9. Richard Koman. The Scent of Information. *Webreview*, May 15, 1998. Available at http://www.webreview.com/1998/05_15/strategists/05_15_98_1.shtml (accessed August 1, 2004).

10. Marcia J. Bates. The Design of Browsing and Berrypicking Techniques for the Online Search Interface. *Online Review*, 13 (5), October 1989, 409–24.

11. Jared M. Spool, Tara Scanlon, Will Schroeder, Carolyn Snyder, and Terri DeAngelo. *Web Site Usability: A Designer's Guide*. San Francisco: Morgan Kaufman, 1999.

12. Richard Saul Wurman. Redesign the Data. *Business2.com*, November 28, 2000, 210–22.

13. A Clyde. Ten Things I Hate About ... Web Pages. *Teacher Librarian*, 27 (2), 1999, 58–59. See also J Fairly. The 6 Mistakes of Highly Ineffective Websites. *Bank Marketing*, 32 (2), 2000, 28–29.

14. Web site analysis tools include Funnel Web Professional, HitBox Pro, NetTracker, SuperStats Professional, and WebTrends Log Analyzer. For current product reviews and a list of new competing products, check http://www.zdnet.com.

15. Available at: http://www.useit.com/papers/heuristic/heuristic_list.html (accessed August 1, 2004).

16. Roger Black. *Web Sites That Work*. San Jose, CA: Adobe Press, 1997.

17. A. Hill. Top 5 Reasons Your Customers Abandon Their Shopping Carts. *Smart Business*, 14 (3), 2001, 80–84; Spool et al.*Web Site Usability.*

18. Kristin Antelman. Getting Out of the HTML Business: The Database-Driven Web Site Solution. *Information Technology and Libraries*, 18 (4), December 1999, 176–81.

19. Thomas P. Truner and Lise Brackbill. Rising to the Top: Evaluating the Use of the HTML META Tag to Improve Retrieval of World Wide Web Documents Through Internet Search Engines. *LRTS*, 42 (4), October 1998, 258–71.

20. Jakob Nielsen. *Homepage Usability: 50 Websites Deconstructed.* Indianapolis, IN: New Riders, 2002.

21. World Wide Web Consortium. *Checklist of Checkpoints for Web Content Accessibility Guidelines 1.0.* Available at: Web site: http://www.w3.org/TR/1999/ WAI-WEBCONTENT-19990505/full-checklist (accessed October 30, 2003).

22. Michael Hudson of the San Francisco Public Library prepared this section of a technology plan.

23. Susan McMullen. (2001). Usability testing in a library Web site redesign project. *Reference Services Review,* 29 (1), 7–22.

24. Nancy Everhart. Web Page Evaluation Worksheet. *Emergency Librarian*, 25 (5), May–June 1998, 22.

25. Alison J. Head & Associates. Usability Study Report: Usability Testing of San Francisco Public Library's Existing Web Site. July 2002.

26. John Kupersmith. *Library Terms That Users Understand.* 2003. Available at: http://www.jkup.net/terms.html (accessed August 1, 2004).

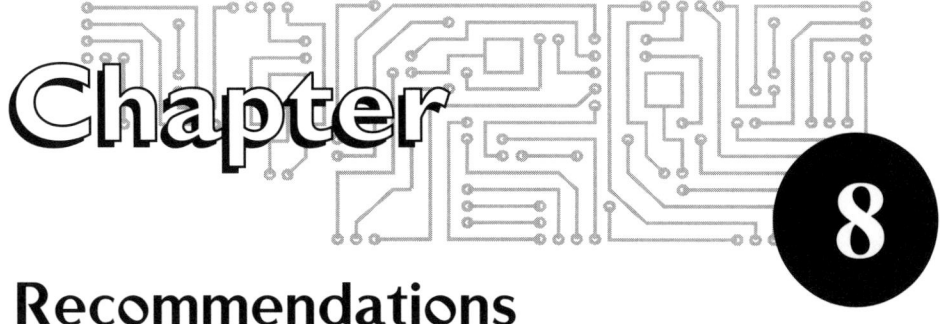

Chapter 8

Recommendations

> *Increasingly, the goal of systems is not to automate, but to enable human collaboration, judgement, and the creation of new value.*—Ethel Himmel and William James Wilson[1]

This is the section of the technology plan where everything comes together. The goal is to develop a plan of action that is cognizant of the needs of the library's customers and assists the library in moving toward achieving its vision of the future.

Thus, this chapter presents a list of the proposed enhancements, upgrades, replacements, and, perhaps, new systems together with a budget, an estimate of the likely costs and benefits for each recommendation, and a suggested implementation time line. The implementation time line must be realistic given the library's available resources yet still reflect the need to move ahead with some speed since technology is constantly changing.

The recommendations should cover the same topics covered in earlier sections of the plan—namely, physical facilities, network infrastructure, servers, desktops, the automated library information system, software for desktops, technical support, and staff skills. A library might want to separate the recommendations into two broad groups: the systematic renewal of technology and innovation-based recommendations. The recommendations that follow from an innovation (whether technology or a library service) should explicitly discuss the positive and negative impacts on the library's customers as the result of the introduction of the innovation.

In addition to a suggested time line, the plan should include a budget for each recommendation. Remember that as funds become available it should be clear what has a higher priority. That is not to say that the plan should be rigid, and as opportunities arise, through the availability of funds via grants or gifts, the library should have the flexibility to seize upon them.

It is also important to recognize that some recommendations are dependent upon other recommendations being implemented first. For example, it may be necessary to enhance and upgrade the bandwidth of the library's LAN so that audio and video files can be listened to and/or viewed at the desktop workstation. In some cases, it may be necessary to upgrade the NIC on some devices so that they can take advantage of the higher network speeds.

One of the first steps in formulating an action plan is to determine what interdependencies exist between each of the various recommendations. Remember that the recommendations were identified earlier when you prepared an assessment of the current environment and examined the usability of the library's Web site.

Once the interdependencies have been identified, it is likely that the recommendations can be logically grouped together into some number of broader themes or topics. In turn, it is then possible to identify the likely priorities among the themes and to determine the total costs for each theme.

It is important to attempt to determine the benefits associated with each recommendation. The cost of a technology does not equate with its benefits. The benefits, from the perspective of the library's customers or staff members, may be more than, equal to, or less than the cost of a technology. Focusing on the benefits of a technology will help the library determine the relative rank order of the recommendations. That is, the cost-benefit ratio for some recommendations will be better than others. Recommendations with a better cost-benefit ratio should, in most cases, be ranked higher. However, the ultimate criteria should be the potential impacts on the library's customers.

And of course, each of the recommendations should identify its annual operating or maintenance costs. In some cases, a seemingly affordable solution will carry much higher annual operating costs (maintenance and update contracts).

Another, often overlooked, factor is that new technologies or new releases of an existing technology can have a steep learning curve. Thus staff must be afforded the opportunity to attend training sessions and have an opportunity to practice so that they will become proficient with the new technology.

One tool that can assist in the development of recommendations is to determine what impact a proposed new application, new service, or enhancement will have on the library. As shown in Figure 8.1, the number of people that may use or be affected by technology can range from a few to hundreds or thousands. In addition, the accessible data or information may be restricted or made broadly available.

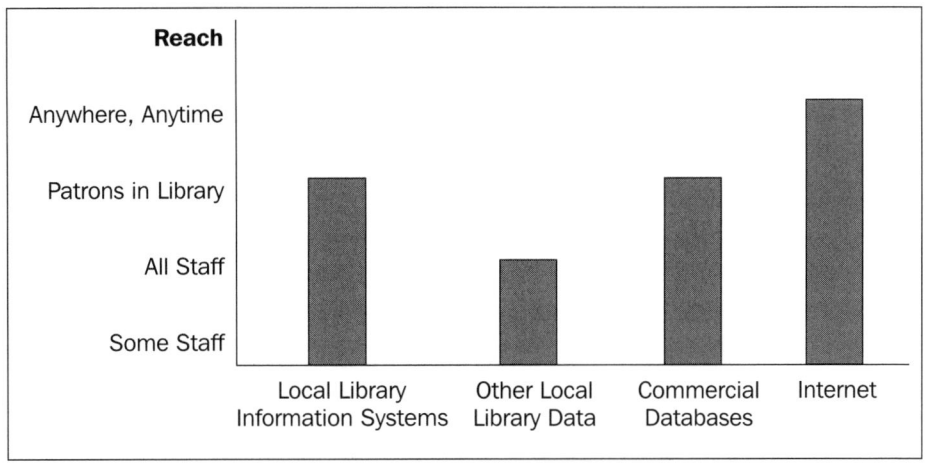

Figure 8.1. Reach and Breadth

The local library information system includes modules used by staff (for example, circulation, acquisitions, serials control, cataloging, and so forth) as well as the library's online catalog. Other local library data might include the library's accounting system, local newspaper index, pathfinders, and so on. The number of commercial databases that the library might have licensed will range from one or two to many. Providing access to the Internet for the library's customers from workstations located in the library is the broadest form of providing access to information. Staff involved with the acquisitions module illustrate that the reach and breadth are limited when compared to a library customer who can access the library's catalog and other commercial databases from any location and at any time during the day or night.

Replicating Figure 8.1 for your library will allow the decision makers to better understand the number of people that will be affected by an investment in a new application or equipment or by upgrading existing equipment or software.

One of the implications of providing anywhere, anytime access to the library's catalog and other resources is that the supporting infrastructure must be very reliable and sufficiently robust to handle the anticipated volume of transactions.

Another important consideration in helping to establish a priority among the various recommendations is to judge the impact that each recommendation will have on meeting the library's vision and objectives.

Once priorities have been established, it is helpful to present the information in a consistent format. Priorities can be sorted into three to five groups (very high to very low). Topics that should be addressed include

- A description of the category of recommendations;
- A listing of the specific recommendations;

- For each recommendation, an indication of its type—new software application, new equipment;
- The costs associated with each recommendation (and interdependency among recommendations);
- The benefits associated with the set of recommendations;
- A recommended schedule or time line to implement the recommendations; and
- An assessment of each recommendation to identify the degree to which staff may need specific training to use new technology.

One effective way to link the proposed action with the corresponding benefits is to use a two-column chart, as shown below:

In the next [time frame], the library will: *Which will result in:*
The action or recommendation   The associated benefits

After the presentation of the recommendations, it is helpful to provide a table that summarizes them. In addition, a table that summarizes the costs for the recommendations, perhaps subdivided into the subtotals for each set of recommendations, will also be helpful to the reader of the plan.

The recommendations should also address the implications for library staff members. Some of the staff may need to attend classes to upgrade their skills prior to a set of recommendations being implemented. In short, the recommendations must be carefully considered, and anything that might inhibit the successful implementation of a specific recommendation or a set of recommendations must be identified as a part of the plan.

Budgeting for technology in a resource-scarce environment can be a real challenge. A library should be spending about 70 to 75 percent of its technology budget on "ongoing costs" such as training, technology upgrades, maintenance, and staff support. The reason is that while a library can have a lot of the "latest and greatest" technologies, if the system is down or no one knows how to use it, the technology's value to the library is negligible.

Sample Section from a Technology Plan

Recommendations[2]

Introduction

The current network infrastructure, when it was implemented two years ago, was considered advanced technology for that time. It has served the library very well, connecting users to the Internet, transferring small to medium-sized files, mostly text files, across the network lines. But many changes have occurred in the last two years, and technology lends itself to the way information delivery operates. It has become standard practice that larger files, such as electronic books, digital images, etc., are transferred electronically across the network. To continue to fulfill its mission as the resource center for information, the library needs to continuously rejuvenate all parts of its technological structure, which includes the network infrastructure, the servers, the computer workstations, and staff skills. The advancement of technology means enhancing or upgrading the system and staff skills.

Network Infrastructure

For the network infrastructure, it is recommended that

1. The library replace all the CAT5 network cables, used for connecting workstations to servers, with fiber optic cables.
2. The cable replacement would yield a faster network connection speed from 100 megabytes per second (Mbps) to 1 gigabytes per second (Gbps).
3. The Library add another wireless network hub to provide additional lines for wireless network connection within the library.
4. As budget allows, the college's fractional DS3 bandwidth be upgraded to full T3 bandwidth.

These recommendations should be forwarded to the district's IT department, which is responsible for the districtwide network infrastructure

Servers

The assessment leads to the following recommendations:

1. **Server 1:** the server for LIS Voyager system, Sun Microsystems Ultra 60, with UNIX operating system. At this point, there is no recommendation for major change to this server.
   - Hardware-wise, this machine is still operating in good standing with only 40 percent capacity; it was purchased with careful planning to last five years, and it should last for another two years without major problem.
   - The software, currently Voyager version 2001.1, should be upgrade to the newer version as soon as that new version is free of bugs.
   - The plan for the operating system (OS) upgrade for this server must wait for the new release of the Voyager system that is compatible with the new version of OS.

- The cost of software and the OS upgrade is incorporated in the current annual maintenance contract.
- Currently the library pays $ 13,200 per year for software maintenance and $2,160 for hardware maintenance, a total of $15,360.

Although there is no immediate need to change the current LIS because its current contract lasts two more years, the library department should begin its selection process for a new system now. Shopping for a LIS is a complicated process. It involves conducting a self-study to determine goals, identifying and documenting the library's needs, evaluating alternatives, and writing a request for proposal (RFP) to send out to vendors. Next, it is necessary to evaluate the various systems to determine which will best fit the needs and goals of the college. The entire process involves most staff members and takes a considerable amount of time. The system selection process should factor the costs of staff training and the data migration process into the budget.

2. **Server 2:** COMPAQ Proliant 6000, running Windows NT
   - This old machine needs to be taken off the network and replaced. Since the library has on hand a Dell P3 PowerEdge 1500SC server, it is ideal to replace the COMPAQ Proliant 6000 with this new machine; and it should be done soon.
   - The Windows 2000 O.S. for the Dell server should be upgraded to Window XP when it becomes available through districtwide licensing.
   - Since the library currently owns this Dell server, there is no extra cost involved with the replacement plan, except the in-house staff time.

3. **Server 3:** COMPAQ Proliant ML370 proxy server. This fairly new machine does not need much attention at this point. It probably only needs upgrading of its Windows 2000 O.S. to Windows XP when it is available.

Computer Workstations

As the Library is preparing to embark on the adventure of providing the video streaming option to students, staff, and faculty, it is necessary to ensure that the equipment is capable of handling the task.

As mentioned in the previous part, the student computer workstations are composed of several different models because they were purchased at different times. Therefore, the recommendations must be specific to each group.

BI Classroom

The 21 Pentium III machines are good for classroom use. With a 20 GB hard drive, 256 MB memory, and 1GHz speed, they are still powerful machines. They only need to upgrade to Win XP OS.

There should be a plan for replacing the current network wiring with wireless network, and looking into laptops for the next replacement, which should occur in the next two years. Although the wireless connection would have a negative impact on the network communication speed by lowering the bandwidth, it will add flexibility to the services. With wireless workstations, bibliographic instruction does not have to be in a designated room; it can be relocated to another area of the library as needed, or to a regular classroom in another building, if the room is equipped with wireless setting.

Laptops

The 16 wireless laptops that are available for two-hour checkout are very popular. The laptops are constantly in use when the library is open. Very often there are more requests than computers available. Based on this heavy usage, it is recommended that:

- The laptops be kept up-to-date with the technology and upgraded to Windows XP OS as well as XP Microsoft Office. The upgrade should be scheduled during the period when the library is closed within the next six months, either during the inter-session or over spring break. The only cost involved with this upgrade plan is the technical support staff time.

- For popularity reasons, the library should acquire more laptops to offer to students.

The Reference Area

This area contains the largest number of computer workstations, with different hardware models, speeds, hard drive capacities, and memory spaces, and also different operating systems. The recommendations are as follows:

- **Hardware**: All machines should be brought up to meet a minimum standard of Pentium III with 256 MB of RAM. This upgrade plan can be accomplished by first replacing the old USMACH Pentium I machines that have only 64 MHz speed with the Dell Pentium III machines that the library recently inherited from the electronics department. Second, more memory (RAM) should be added to the machines that have less then 256 MB.

- **Operating system**: All machines should be upgraded to at least Windows 2000 and at best Windows XP. Because many of these machines are still running Windows NT and are no longer on the vendor's support list, the upgrade should be implemented as soon as possible. The cost of the OS licensing is covered by the district budget as a part of the districtwide licensing agreement.

Staff Machines

Although the model range of staff computer workstations is not as wide as the student workstations, the majority need to be upgraded. Fifty percent of the staff machines only have 128 MB of RAM; they should be increased to 256 MB to improve performance. Another necessary improvement for these machines is the OS upgrade. Most of them are still running Windows NT and need to be moved on to Windows XP.

Through the generosity of a local electronics company, the library recently received a gift package of memory chips: 40 pieces of 256 MB RAM each. This donation would allow the implementation of the memory upgrade process to begin as soon as the technical support staff member can schedule his time. And hopefully the memory upgrade will be followed by the OS upgrade.

Software

The recommendations for software on the computer workstations for both library staff and patrons follow:

- The LIS Voyager client software must be upgraded along with the software upgrade on the server.

- OCLC cataloging utilities software should keep up with the latest available version.

- The Baker&Taylor program should keep up with the latest available version.

- For Integrated Fund Accounting System (IFAS) and the Admission Record programs, the library needs to follow the district upgrade planning and procedure.

- The current Microsoft Office 2000 software should be upgraded to XP as soon as the district makes it available.

- For Internet access, the library should use the newer versions of the Internet Explorer and Netscape programs.

Printers and Other Peripherals

In the area of technology equipment, printers, scanners, and barcode readers do not require major attention at this point. Perhaps establishing a regular maintenance schedule would be sufficient to maintain the equipment's operation. On the other hand, the students' printer, the pay printer that connects to a four-year-old PC, should be upgraded. An outside company that also provides photocopy equipment for student use in the library owns the whole print station. The printer itself does not need replacement, but the PC that manages the print process needs to be replaced with a newer machine.

Headsets for the computer workstations are necessary in the near future, especially when the video streaming service becomes available for student use. Providing headsets for librarians on duty is a plus for reference services.

Staff Skills

It is important that the library staff update their technology skills on a regular basis to perform their duties effectively. The current practice of computer skills training provided by the college on a regular basis, and the training for other skills specific to the library, is necessary and should continue. The training can be arranged as part of in-service training during the intersession period when there are no classes on campus. Also, with every LIS system upgrade there should be special training for staff to be informed of new features available in the system.

It is essential that technical support staff stay informed about the new technology development. This process can be accomplished through special training or reading literature in the field.

Summary

The recommendations can be summarized as follows: All workstations' hardware should be at least Pentium II, with 256 MB of RAM and 10 GB of hard drive. They should all have Windows XP or at least 2000 as the operating system, and have the Microsoft Office XP program. There should be a plan for additional wireless laptops and to convert the BI room to a wireless network environment in the next two years. On the server side, besides replacement of the oldest COMPAQ Proliant 6000 with a Dell machine, there is an important task, planning for a new LIS system selection process, which needs to begin now regardless of the budget situation. Staff training should be factored into budget planning.

8—Recommendations

	Recommendations and Time Lines
Dates	**Recommended Actions**
Beginning 2004	• Replace COMPAQ Proliant 6000 server with Dell P3 PowerEdge 1500SC server. • Start gathering thoughts and information on new LIS specification.
Beginning 2004	• Request a replacement of pay printer station with a new PC and latest version of print software.
Starting 2004 continues through the end of 2004	***Student workstations:*** • Phase out old Pentium Is and replace with DELL Pentium III machines. • Upgrade RAM to 256 MB. • Upgrade OS from Win NT to Win 2000/XP. • Upgrade laptops' OS to Win XP. • Add headsets to PCs that can accommodate them. ***Staff machines:*** • Upgrade RAM to 256 MB. • Upgrade OS from Win NT to Win 2000/XP. • Add headsets for librarians at the reference desk. ***Software programs:*** • Upgrade MS Office from 2000 to XP on all workstations.
Mid-2004	• Upgrade OS on COMPAQ Proliant ML370 proxy server from Win 2000 to XP. • Upgrade Voyager system from 2001.1 to newer available release.
2005	***BI classroom:*** • Replace existing network with wireless. • Replace existing PCs with laptops. • Add more wireless laptops (if budget allows). • Propose to ITS: replace CAT5 network cables with fiber optic cables (propose to IT department).
2005	• Target for installation of a new LIS.

Notes

1. Ethel Himmel and William James Wilson. *Planning for Results: A Public Library Transformation*. Chicago: American Library Association, 1998.
2. This section of the technology plan was prepared by Noreth Men.

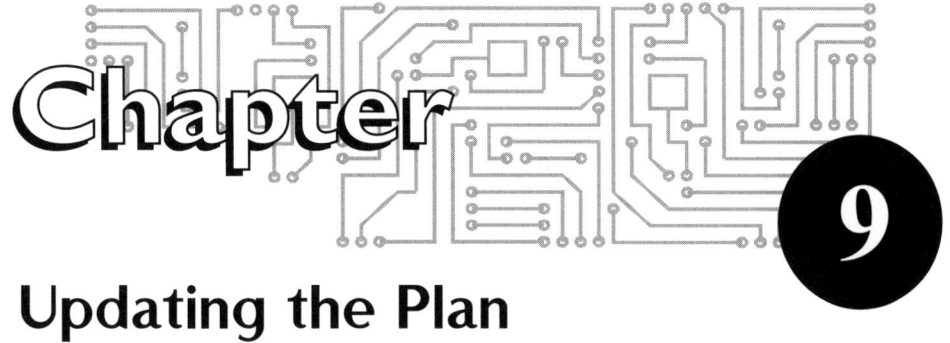

Chapter 9

Updating the Plan

> *Information technology strategic planning is a dynamic process that seeks to help the library transform from its current state toward its future vision.*—Jan Baltzer[1]

Any technology plan should include a section for ongoing monitoring and assessment of the implementation of the various recommendations, as well as appraising the continued relevance of the plan itself. The section should have a specified methodology for regular evaluations and, as necessary, revising the plan when needed.

Subjecting the technology plan to an annual review, typically in concert with the budget preparation process, will ensure that the library is not overlooking an important technology that could boost staff productivity or provide improved services to the library's customers. The constant of technology is change, and nothing speaks quite so clearly as a technology plan that is no longer current or relevant.

A technology plan with a planning horizon of more than two to three years is clearly not grounded in reality. While the mission and vision of the library may not change, the strategies and enabling technologies most likely will be changing, and the library's stakeholders and funding decision makers need to know the realities that are facing libraries today. For most libraries, the focus on high-quality service to customers and increased user satisfaction is a constant; the ways in which service is and can be delivered are certainly evolving and changing.

The assessment of the technology plan involves two basic activities. The first is monitoring the progress of implementation of the recommendations stated in the plan, especially as new funding opportunities may arise. Each recommendation should have a time frame associated with when implementation will have been completed and the library's management team should have assigned responsibility for the completion of each task to a specific individual. The library might wish to develop an implementation plan tracking chart as illustrated in Table 9.1.

The second basic activity is developing a plan for staying relatively current with technology trends. It may be that selected individuals will be responsible for reading specific journals—within and outside the library field. Articles of interest can then be shared with the team that is assigned to the evaluation of the technology plan itself. Attending appropriate sessions at professional conferences will also help, as will networking with fellow librarians in other libraries.

Table 9.1. Sample Implementation Plan Tracking Chart

Activity	Person Responsible	Scheduled Completion Date	Dependent on What Other Activities	Comments
Upgrade LAN to 100 Mbps	T. Johnson	March 2005	Upgrade speed of Internet link	
Install new Network Interface Cards (NIC) in all devices connected to the LAN	T. Johnson and R. Markel	February 2005	None	
Install new Web server	J. Samuels	April 2005	Upgrade speed of Internet link	
Install new router and firewall for new Web server	J. Samuels	April 2005		Router back-ordered

Unmistakably, information technology is advancing at a rapid pace. Consistently evaluating and updating the plan is crucial to staying on track. Not every recommendation can be completed in a single fiscal year. Thus, progress reports should be made to the library's management team on a regular, scheduled basis (e.g., quarterly).

In addition to progress reports, an annual review will help remind the library's management team (and a technology planning committee—if such a committee is) of what progress has been made and enable it to determine what remains to be accomplished. Ideally, the plan's review will be used as a guide to identify what needs to be accomplished during the upcoming fiscal year. Once the library adopts the revision, it allows the library to focus its efforts and funds on using technology as another means of improving the services to its customers.

The library may wish to establish a standing technology planning committee to assist the library's management team in coping with the constantly changing nature of technology. Some libraries have found the use of a standing committee to be an effective way of involving those who are interested in technology. In the following sections we offer suggestions as to the How, Who, etc. of evaluation.

How

The technology planning committee must stay informed about the state of the automation industry; one way of doing that is through reading literature in the library field. *Library Journal*, in its April 1 issue, publishes an annual review called "Automated System Marketplace," which discusses the previous year's major events in the field. Another way to stay informed is to ask questions and discuss concerns with colleagues either through e-mail or online discussion group. Besides staying informed about technology trends, the committee should

- Develop a three- to four-year technology plan; review it every year and update as needed. Make sure that the plan presents clear goals so the decision makers can see the big picture for the department as a whole rather than just a list of hardware and software.

- Recognize that it may not be possible to achieve the goals in one big step, but rather get partial solutions in incremental phases, which lead the library in the right direction toward an accomplishment of long-term goals. For instance, in terms of budget, it is not possible for the library to upgrade or replace the computer workstations all at the same time. However, it is possible to split them into multiple groups and select one group at a time to be the target for upgrading or replacing.

- Set realistic goals. Rather than making a high-tech wish list, produce an updated plan that shows an incremental growth of computer, communications networks, and other peripheral equipment that will be needed to support the library's goals. Remember that technology is simply a tool to help the library provide service to its customers. Compare what is, after a year, with what was proposed. Are the goals still realistic? Has the world outstripped the library's plan? In what respects? Are the original premises still valid? Have there been any earth-shattering changes in Internet technologies, in funding, etc.?

- Keep up with the trends of what's available and what's new in the market.
- Determine what was on the wish list. Is it still to be wished for? Should it graduate to a goal?

Who

The library technology planning should be developed and maintained by a technology planning committee. The best strategy for keeping the technology plan current begins with the selection of a committee that represents those who would be responsible for implementing the plan. The committee might consist of members who represent the following functional areas:

- **Systems**: Include at least the systems librarian who might be the committee's chairperson, and at most the technical support staff that can provide assistance with the detail of the current technology status.
- **Cataloging and acquisition:** It is important to include a representative from cataloging and the acquisitions group. This group interfaces with technology in the area of incoming data traffic flow.
- **Reference:** A representative from the reference area is essential to the committee. This area has direct interface with the end-user side of the systems through the online catalog. The group, which consists of all librarians whose duties are helping users, can provide feedback from the end-user point of view.
- **Circulation:** This group also has direct interface with the end-user side of the systems, but from the staff point of view. A representative from this group would provide a perspective point of view of technology that is different from the online catalog and report any problems with or challenges facing the existing library information system and the associated infrastructure.
- **IT department:** It may not be necessary to have an IT person serve on the committee on a permanent basis. But it is valuable to have someone from the IT department who can provide information concerning the planned changes for the infrastructure side of the technology. In addition, this individual can provide a welcome nonlibrary perspective on trends in the information technology arena.

Summary

It is important that the library keep its plan current with technology as well as with its needs. Technology planning should be about how technology can add value to the library and the people it serves.

What follows is a sample of an executive summary prepared for a community college library; it is included to provide an example of a readable summary.

Executive Summary[2]

The purposes of this technology plan are to evaluate and assess the current state of the library's technology and decide what to update or replace. Technology plays an important role in providing library services; therefore, it is equally important to be sure that the library's technology is here to enrich, not hinder, library services.

The following is a summary from each of the eight sections of this technology plan.

Description of the Library

The Anywhere City College Library is part of a large, complex organization that shares the campus mission of working together, pursuing excellence, and inspiring achievement. The library consists of two departments, the library and the instructional media department (nonprint library). The library seeks to support the educational goals set by the campus by providing staff that exceed Title V expectations, a collection of approximately 71,343 titles with 4.5 percent growth in the year 2001–2002, and an approximate annual circulation of 323,602. The technology environment is currently good, because a new integrated library system replaced the old one and all staff computers were replaced to accommodate the new system in 2002. Unfortunately, the Library Division budget (set by the campus administrators) does not allow the division to budget for appropriate technology needs, and any proposed changes must be included in the campus plan. Once all division unit plans are complete, the campus budget committee decides which divisions get funding.

Challenges Facing the Library

It is agreed among staff that the number one challenge is money, which becomes more of a challenge during years the California state budget has problems. Other challenges include no technology portion in the budget set by campus administrators, no easy way to get new technology incorporated quickly, and that campus instructional technology staff are not as accessible as the library would like them to be. On the other hand, the dedicated library staff work hard to maintain efficient library services to all library patrons in spite of any and all the challenges the library faces.

Current Technology Environment

Patrons will always ask for more technological resources than the library can supply. However, the resources the library currently uses are fairly new, ranging in purchase date from 1999 to 2002. All machines that required new technology to run library software have newer equipment. The campus provides all the necessary software on all staff machines, and all student machines are equipment with software that follows campus curriculum. Technical support is well taken care of by campus and district IT staff, and library staff have numerous training opportunities to keep most of their skills current.

Assessment of Current Technology Environment

The library currently has a good (although not cutting edge) technology environment. In the future, technology will need to be upgraded or replaced, but the current state of library technology should serve the library well until 2005, when equipment warranties expire and the computers may not run what they will need in 2005. Unfortunately, the library does not have much control over upgrading technology (no division technology budget or access to network resources without information technology staff approval). Currently the district and campus handle most technology issues. The library can only look into innovative ways of using what the district provides and into influencing campus decisions that affect the library's technology needs.

Analysis of Options

This section looks at the different options the library has when purchasing an integrated library system. Positive and negative aspects of purchasing an in-house system, a shared system, and an ISP have been evaluated. District policy dictates that all campuses must share the same ILS, so an in-house system is not possible. The district pays for the current shared ILS; sometime in the future the libraries in the district may want to suggest using an ISP instead of the shared system, because it may save the district money. Using an ISP means no server costs and less time that district IT staff devote to maintenance.

Library Web Site

The library Web site is important because it allows library patrons to access the library off campus and during closed hours. It serves as an information source for the library as well as a gateway to the OPAC and online databases. The Web site was evaluated and was then compared to the other campus in the district using the same Web site evaluations. The conclusion of the evaluation proposed the following no-cost adjustments to the Web site:

- Change background color (to white preferably).
- Post planned revision schedule.

- All pages or sections of pages should have author, author's title, and author's e-mail address.

- Consider using two frames (one for a menu bar and one for main content). Look at any of the other campus Web sites for examples.

- Make the first page a home page that organizes the information in an appropriate fashion.

- Add a Web site search engine.

- Add subject pathfinders for frequently asked for research topics.

- Add a text-only version.

- Test final page in both Netscape and Explorer to be sure it can be viewed properly in both.

- Reconsider the use of burgundy headers. It is close to the color red, which visually impaired people have problems viewing.

- Make current news easier to identify. A short explanation of *The Reader* being the library's newsletter that includes library news or current events may do.

Recommendations

Overall there are not many technology recommendations to currently suggest for this draft of the technology plan. Other than updating the Web site, this plan also recommends updating this technology plan on a yearly basis in the fall semester so the information can be included in the spring unit plans (which happen to be a requirement to get funding for technology upgrades and/or replacements). This plan further recommends that library staff get involved in the shared governance committees the campus allows all staff to volunteer for. Participating on the committee will help library staff learn about and influence campus decisions that affect technology and may even help them get proposals funded.

Plan for Revisions

This technology plan recommends revising the plan on a yearly basis, during the fall semester. A committee with the dean of library services as head, who invites campus IT staff to sit in on the revision meetings, will be the most effective way to revise the technology plan. It is important the technology plan stay up to date for planning purposes, which will result in getting the funding support needed to carry out the approved proposals.

Notes

1. Jan A. Baltzer. Consider the Four-Legged Stool as You Plan for Information Technology. *Computers in Libraries*, 20 (4), April 2000, 42–45.
2. This executive summary was prepared by Dena Martin.

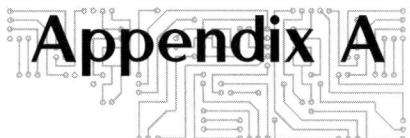

Appendix A

Forms

The three forms included in this appendix will assist the library in preparing a technology plan. They include an inventory of current equipment and software that is installed in the library, an assessment of the technology-related skills of library staff members, and an assessment of what technology may be needed to upgrade a variety of services offered by the library.

Form A. Current Technology Inventory

Item	Quantity	Description
Desktop devices		
Dumb terminals		
Personal computers		
Speed of processor		
Amount of RAM		
Disk space		
CD-ROM/DVD drive		
Sound card		
Speakers/headphones		
Desktop software		
Operating system		
Internet browser		
Library information system		
Other application software		
Servers		
Processor type and speed		
Amount of RAM		
Disk space		
Operating system		
Printers		
Manufacturer and model		
Number of pages per minute		
Black and white/color		

Form A. Current Technology Inventory

Item	Quantity	Description
Local area network		
Hub		
Total ports		
Total unused ports		
Network typology		
Speed		
Type of cable to desktops		
Network operating system		
Wide area network		
Routers/bridges		
Manufacturer and model		
Speed		
Bandwidth to ISP		
Leased lines		
Access to the library's catalog		
Via the Internet		
Dialup lines		
Cable or broadcast television		
Videoconferencing		
Satellite downlink		

Form B. Evaluation of Staff Skills

Skill Area	Current Level of Staff Skills	Level of Skills Needed	Number of Staff and Hours of Training Needed
Windows Skills			
Basic			
Average			
Advanced			
Web-based Browser Skills			
Basic			
Average			
Advanced			
Automated Library Information System			
Basic			
Average			
Advanced			
Office Suite (Word Processing, Spreadsheet, etc.)			
Basic			
Average			
Advanced			
E-mail			
Basic			
Average			
Advanced			

Form B. Evaluation of Staff Skills

Skill Area	Current Level of Staff Skills	Level of Skills Needed	Number of Staff and Hours of Training Needed
Commercial Application (Name)			
Basic			
Average			
Advanced			
Commercial Application (Name)			
Basic			
Average			
Advanced			
Commercial Application (Name)			
Basic			
Average			
Advanced			

Form C. Technology Assessment

Consider what telecommunications connectivity, computer hardware, and software are needed for each existing or proposed service. What is needed may be something new, or it may be an upgrade to the existing technology mix within your library.

	What Telecommunication Connectivity Is Needed?	What Computer and Peripheral Equipment Is Needed?	What Software Is Needed?
Service A			
Service B			
Service C			
Service D			
Service E			
Service F			
Service G			
Service H			
Service I			
Service J			
Service K			
Service L			
Service M			

Appendix B

Analysis of Library Information System Options

For most libraries, the basic components of a library information system include:

- Acquisitions
- Serials
- Cataloging
- Circulation
    - Interlibrary loan (ILL)
    - Document delivery
- Ordering/receiving (books and serials)
- Management reporting
- Administration

The reasons a library may be making inquires into new vendors/systems can include, but are certainly not limited to,

- **Problems with support:** Response to problems is incomplete, tardy, or nonexistent.
- **Insufficient processing capabilities:** The database or volume of transactions has outgrown the system capabilities.
- **Vendor business problems:** A vendor goes under or is acquired by a company not interested in the library marketplace.

- **Technical issues:** The vendor will not migrate in a timely manner from an outdated operating system, database, or computer programming language.

- **Technically outdated:** The vendor continues to rely on outdated software tools and languages.

Three options are available for a library to have access to an automated library information system. These include in-house, shared/consortium, and application service provider (ASP) solutions.[1]

Definitions

In-house systems can be either a turnkey automated system for all library functions or implemented on an as-needed basis. In-house systems are completely run/managed by the purchasing library, and generally the system can be configured (parameters or options) to meet the individual needs of the institution. As an example, a library could choose to implement the circulation module initially, and for whatever reason, leave the other modules until a later time. A majority of all types of libraries have chosen the in-house option. Vendors active in the library information system marketplace are reviewed in an annual article published each year in April by *Library Journal*.

Shared systems (the terms *shared* and *consortium* are interchangeable) are used to run multiple, geographically and operationally separate libraries that typically share computing resources, software, and databases while maintaining separate user interfaces and accounting processes. A number of libraries have chosen this option, and while most cooperative members are similar types of libraries, there are examples of successful multitype library consortiums that share an automated system.

It should also be mentioned that two additional benefits of shared systems, improved access and shared resources, are greatly improved in the case of a network of regional libraries.

Application service providers (ASPs) offer a solution in which the customer does not pay for the software in a traditional up-front manner, nor does it pay for the costs of hardware or maintenance. Rather, all costs are bundled into a fixed monthly fee, and the vendor retains complete ownership of and responsibility for the hardware, software, and operation of the system; the services are in effect leased to the library or consortium. The ASP provider hosts the software, hardware, and database and in turn runs the library's system on remote hardware, again bundled into the monthly costs.

Strengths and Weaknesses

The following sections provide an overview of the issues, strengths, and weakness of the three options.

Control of Software

One of the obvious concerns is the issue of how much control the library has over the ownership and functionality of the software. These concerns are summarized in the following table.

System	In-House	Consortium	ASP
Strengths	• Library owns license to the software and should also have access to the source code should vendor exit business. • Generally customizable and configurable to meet existing and future needs. • Can build/modify software if vendor unable/unwilling. • Innovations encouraged and benefit the library.	• Shared software dilutes control—ownership and therefore changes negotiated among owners. • Customizable and configurable to the needs of all consortia members. • Can still build/maintain but limited by consortium decision-making processes. • Innovations encouraged and benefit the consortium—especially those who don't partake in the development process.	• Vendor usually responsive to requests for modifications or enhancements. • Least expensive—software never purchased. • Industry standards should be in place for operating systems, hardware, and software. • Maintenance, upgrades, and service done at remote site by vendor. • Library retains ownership of database.
Weaknesses	• Vendor may not support client-made changes. • Inherently complex set-up and installation.	• Vendor may not support client-made changes. • Middle ground costs between stand-alone in-house and ASP.	• Vendor can choose how and when to modify software. • No ownership of software. • Ability to configure/customize the software is less clear (not in the interest of the ASP).

Support Staff

The number of staff within a library needed to support a system will vary, depending upon the option chosen. The number of support staff obviously affects the budget.

System	In-House	Consortium	ASP
Strengths	• The vendor has an interest—annual maintenance revenue—to train staff. • Systems librarians can bridge many gaps between the user base and the systems providers/vendors. • A systems librarian and trained staff could fill the gaps caused by a vendor going out of business.	• Maintenance is a known, predictable process as in the in-house scenarios. • Systems librarians can bridge many gaps between the user base and the systems providers/vendors.	• Vendor must ensure that the system is stable so that unforeseen maintenance does not erode its profits. • If the vendor departs the business, the user is left with no recourse to keep the system up and running. • Small to medium-sized library solution.
Weaknesses	• Gaps that occur when highly trained staff depart will be disruptive to library operations.	• Gaps that occur when highly trained staff depart remain highly disruptive to library operations. • Adding consortium members may cause short-term impacts to operations.	• Less of a need to have systems support staff at library. • Relies on management skills of ASP account/system management.

Infrastructure

Depending upon the option chosen, the library may need to install and maintain a robust information technology infrastructure. In all cases, the library will be responsible for supporting a stable local area network with sufficient bandwidth as well as all of the desktop computers and other devices connected to the LAN.

System	In-House	Consortium	ASP
Strengths	• Significant user base can help with support and other issues.	• An active customer base can help with support and other issues.	• None of the infrastructure owned by the library.
Weaknesses	• Highly complex combinations of server, database, network, and desktop interaction and interdependency. • Complexity and reliance on more than one service provider increases risk. • Can drive development of new infrastructure.	• Combined systems and tele-communications complexity. • Highly complex combinations of server, database, network, and desktop interaction and interdependency.	• Telecommunications is the single point of failure. • Reliant on vendor to develop new infrastructure. • While application user groups can still support requests for enhancements, not clear if ASP users are equally organized.

Implementation, Time Frames, and Conversion Cost

Each option has different implementation issues and installation time frames. The costs of moving from one system to the next system will vary, often significantly.

System	In-House	Consortium	ASP
Strengths	• More probable that the software can be configured to work with existing database.	• Longest time, most complex to implement due to the group decision-making process. • More probable that the software can be configured to work with existing database.	• The low-cost, fast start-up solution. • Probable that software can be configured to work with existing databases (MARC, etc.).
Weaknesses	• Highly complex and expensive up-front costs/service. • Considerable time to implement and configure. • May need to run parallel systems at startup. • Extended time frames to get up and running . • All start-up costs "lost" when/if library abandons vendor.	• Highly complex and expensive up-front costs/service. • Extended time frames to get up and running. • All start-up costs "lost" when/if library abandons vendor. • May need to run parallel systems at startup.	• All start-up costs "lost" when/if library abandons vendor. • "One-off" systems such as materials booking may need to be modified. • May need to run parallel systems at startup.

Implementation Cost Issues

The costs for each option will vary as shown in the following table.

System	In-House	Consortium	ASP
Strengths	• Complexity should deliver a system designed to meet the library's specific needs.	• Complexity should deliver a system meeting many individual library needs while compromising the fewest consortium members' needs.	• The low-cost, fast start-up solution.
Weaknesses	• Extended time frames to get up and running. • All start-up costs "lost" when/if library abandons vendor. • Highly complex and expensive up-front costs/service.	• Extended time frames to get up and running. • All start-up costs "lost" when/if library abandons vendor. • Highly complex and expensive up-front costs/service.	• All start-up costs "lost" when/if library abandons vendor.

Transaction Volumes and Security Issues

System	In-House	Consortium	ASP
Strengths	• The library is responsible for the security of servers and the desktop computers. • Transaction volumes predictable. • Transaction volumes controllable—toggle acquisitions, new collections, etc.	• Larger group of users, more resources for support—mitigation of security problems. • Multiple platforms/users—more redundancy. • Benefit from consortium member cataloging work—grow database using consortium records.	• Security should be a key selling point. • 24/7 service level agreement (SLA) should be a component of system.
Weaknesses	• Limited in-house security services/support. • Single point of failure. • Completely responsible for catalog growth.	• More entry points (physical and logical) for potential security problems. • Transaction volumes less predictable.	• Less familiar with campus computing environments and built-in security issues (campus mischief). • Transaction volumes may incur more expenses—depending on how contracts structured—the library may have to pay for "excessive" or out of contract transaction volume fees.

Cost Analysis

The cost variables shown in the table are designed to illustrate the analysis and evaluation a library should follow when exploring the possible use of the alternatives. Final figures should be obtained from a selected short-list of vendors/systems the library chooses to investigate further.

Component	In-House	Shared	ASP
Hardware	$ 40,000	$ 10,000	-
Software	100,000	25,000	-
Maintenance	25,200	6,300	-
Staff	140,000	115,000	
Telecommunications	-	36,000	$ 36,000
ASP Service	-	-	60,000
Total Costs (Five Years)	$966,000	$796,300	480,000
Average Costs Per Year	$193,200	$159,260	96,000

Assume that four libraries are sharing a system with equal costs. Thus, for example, the cost of $10,000 for hardware is one library's share of the cost. Maintenance costs are assumed to be 18 percent per year. Staff costs include a system manager at $60,000 per year and two systems support staff at $40,000 each per year (for the shared system, two systems support staff plus a one-quarter share of the system manager's salary). A shared system will require leased lines to each library (system is not located in any one of the libraries). The ASP option will, in this case, require the installation of an additional T1 line to connect the ASP vendor to the library.

Thus, the savings from a shared system as well as the ASP option are considerable. However, the strengths and weakness of each option in relationship to overall library operations must be considered in addition to the economic factors. For some libraries, issues such as functionality, service, and support are considered indispensable, so the in-house or shared system option will be selected.

Notes

1. For a further discussion of these options, see chapter 10 in Thomas R. Kochtanek and Joseph R. Matthews. *Library Information Systems: From Library Automation to Distributed Information Access Solutions*. Westport, CT: Libraries Unlimited, 2002. See also Joseph R. Matthews. *Internet Outsourcing Using an Application Service Provider: A How-To-Do-It Manual for Librarians*. New York: Neal-Schuman, 2002.

Index

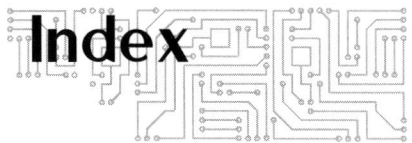

Accountability and Web Services, 51
Amazon.com
   and customer intimacy, 32
   and emerging technologies, 41
Americans with Disabilities Act (ADA), 57
Appendixes in technology plan, 10
"Automated System Marketplace," 113
Automated systems overview
   in technology plan, sample, 22–23

Baltzer, Jan, 111
Barriers to entry to Web services, low, 49
Black, Roger, 88
Blog, defined, 84
Bluetooth, 47
Book Industry Standards Advisory Committee (BISAC), 46
Budget, 102
   description in technology plan, sample, 20

Cerritos (California) Public Library, 51
Challenges facing library, explanation of in technology plan
   defined, 9
   external, 27–30
   internal, 26–27
   sample, 33–38, 115
   strategies for dealing with, 30–33

Chandler (Arizona) Public Library, 51
Clarke, Arthur, 53
Clients/customers
   role in technology planning, 8
Collection size
   description in technology plan, sample, 20–22
Costs, 130–31
   analysis, 133
Current technology environment, assessment of in technology plan. *See also* Technology inventory
   data, 72
      sample, 81
   form, 124
   hardware/operating system
      desktops, 68–69, 77–78 (sample)
      servers, 68, 75–76 (sample)
   network availability, 67–68, 81 (sample)
   network infrastructure, 66–67, 74 (sample)
   physical facilities, 65–66
   software
      desktops, 70, 79–80 (sample)
      library information system, 69–70, 78 (sample)
      librarywide, 70, 79 (sample)
   sample, 73–82
   staff skills, 72–73, 81–82 (sample)
   technical support, 71–72, 81 (sample)

Current technology environment, description of in technology plan, 53
    assessing, 10, 54
    defined, 9
    inventory form, 120–21
    sample, 57–64, 116
Custom integration, 48
Customer intimacy, defined, 32

Data (backups, virus protection), inventorying/assessing, 56, 72
    sample, 81
Data Type Definition (DTD), 45
Dell Computers, 69
    and operational excellence, 32
Description of library in technology plan
    defined, 9
    mission statement, 15–16
    organization of, 13–15
    sample, 16–23, 115
DTD. *See* Data Type Definition
Dublin Core, 44, 46
Dugan, Robert E., 5

Economy, as external challenge, 27–28, 29(fig.)
    sample SWOT analysis of, 35–36
Emerging technologies, description of in technology plan, 41–42
    defined, 9
    peer-to-peer networking, 43–45
    RFID, 51
    TCP/IP, 42–43
    voice and translation capabilities, 47
    Web services, 48–51
    wireless connections, 46–47
    XML, 45–46
Encoded Archival Description (EAD), 35

Ethics, as external challenge, 28, 30(fig.)
    sample SWOT analysis of, 37
Evaluation factors for Web sites
    access, 89
    authority, 89
    content, 88–89
    currency, 88
    experience, 89
    multimedia, 89
    navigation, 89
    treatment, 89
Evaluation of library's Web site in technology plan, 83
    defined, 10
    sample, 90–97, 116–17
    Web site design, 84–90
Everhart, Nancy, 88, 91
Executive summary in technology plan
    defined, 9
    sample, 115–17
Extensible Markup Language (XML), 44, 78, 84
    DTD, 45
    related standards, 45–46
    and SGML, 45

Fast-ethernet local area network (FELAN), 74
Federal Express, and operational excellence, 32
File Transfer Protocol (FTP), 78, 81
Forms
    current technology inventory, 120–22
    staff skills evaluation, 122–23
    technology assessment, 124
Frisch, Max, 41

George, Henry, 65
Google, 28
    and emerging technologies, 41

Hardware/operating system
   inventorying/assessing
      desktops, 55, 68–69, 77–78 (sample)
      servers, 55, 68, 75–76 (sample)
   recommendations for changing
      printers/peripherals, 106–7 (sample)
      servers, 103–4 (sample)
      workstations, 104–6 (sample)
Head, Alison J., & Associates, 95
Helping.org, 10
Hewlett Packard (HP), 69
Himmel, Ethel, 99
Hooker, Richard, 25
HP. *See* Hewlett Packard
Hubbard, Elbert, 13

IBM, 69
IEEE 802.11, 46–47
Industry support for Web services, 50
Information access
   electronic, 8
   intellectual, 8
   physical, 8
Information technology (IT), 23, 71
Information technology (IT) department, 59, 114
Innovative services, defined, 32
Internet
   and emerging technologies, 42
   and Web services, 49
Internet service provider (ISP), 53, 67
Internet Surveys, 10
Internet2, 42
Interoperability of Web services, 49
ISP. *See* Internet service provider

Katz, Stanley M., 83
Kupersmith, John, 95

LAN. *See* Local area network
Law, as external challenge, 28, 30(fig.)
   sample SWOT analysis of, 37
Library director
   role in technology planning, 3, 7
Library Information system options, analysis of, 125–26
   cost analysis, 133
   definitions, 126
   strengths and weaknesses, 127–32
Library Research Planning, 11
Library Technology Planning, 11
"Library Terms That Users Understand," 95
LINC Project, 11
Local area network (LAN), 43, 57, 58, 66, 74, 81, 100

Maricopa County (Arizona) Public Library, 51
Markets, as external challenge, 28, 29(fig.)
   sample SWOT analysis of, 36
Metcalfe's Law, 43
Middleware products, 48
Mission statement
   in description of challenges facing library, sample, 33
   in description of library, 14, 15–16
   sample, 17–19
MODS, 46
Moore's Law, 42, 83

National Center for Technology Planning, 2, 11
Network availability, inventorying/assessing, 55, 67–68
   sample, 81
Network infrastructure
   inventorying/assessing, 54, 66–67, 74 (sample)

and library information system, 129
recommendations for changing, 103 (sample)
Network interface card (NIC), 67, 100
North Central Regional Educational Laboratory, 11
Npower, 11

Objectives
characteristics of (SMART), 6–7
defined, 6
Online public access catalog (OPAC), 16, 22, 23, 34, 55, 56, 60, 67, 70, 79, 84
Operational excellence, defined, 31–32
Orange County (Florida) Public Library, 51
Osten, March, 4

Peer-to-peer networking, 43–45
LANs in, 43
versus client/server computing, 44
Personal digital assistant (PDA), 17, 46, 47, 67
Physical facilities, inventorying/assessing, 54, 65–66
Plan for action in technology plan defined, 10
Politics, as external challenge, 28, 29(fig.)
sample SWOT analysis of, 36–37
Providence (Rhode Island) College, 51

Radio Frequency Identification (RFID), 29, 51
RDF. *See* Resource Description Framework
Recommendations for improving Web site, sample, 95–96

Recommendations in technology plan, 99–102
defined, 10
sample, 102–8, 117
Reliability of Web services, 50
Resource Description Framework (RDF), 44, 46
Resources for planning, 8
Web, 10–12
RFID. *See* Radio Frequency Identification

Santa Clara (California) Public Library, 51
Scalability of Web services, 50
Search engines, 28
Security of Web services, 50
Serials Industry Standards Advisory Committee (SISAC), 46
Simple Mail Transfer Protocol (SMTP), 78, 81
Simple Object Access Protocol (SOAP), 45–46
Society, as external challenge, 28, 30(fig.)
sample SWOT analysis of, 37–38
Software
inventorying/assessing
desktops, 55, 70, 79–80 (sample)
library information system, 55, 69–70, 78 (sample), 127
librarywide, 55, 70, 79 (sample)
recommendations for changing, 106 (sample)
Special Library Association, 11
Speech recognition, 47
Staff
role in technology planning, 7
Staff skills
inventorying/assessing, 56–57, 72–73
form, 122–23
sample, 81–82

recommendations for changing, 107 (sample)
Staffing
  description in technology plan, sample, 19–20
  for library information system, 128
Stakeholders
  role in technology planning, 8
Strategies for dealing with challenges
  customer intimacy, 32
  defined, 30
  interrelationship of, 31(fig.)
  innovative services, 32
  MOST, 31
  operational excellence, 31
  technology-based, 32
Strengths, weaknesses, opportunities, and threats. *See* SWOT analysis
SWOT analysis
  examples of, 34–38
  internal assessment, 26–27
  "TEMPLES" (external assessment), 27–30, examples of, 34–38

TCP/IP. *See* Transmission Control Protocol/Internet Protocol
Tech Soup, 11
TechAtlas, 11
Technical support, inventorying/assessing, 56
  patrons, 71
  sample, 81
  staff, 71–72
Technology, as external challenge, 27, 29(fig.)
  sample SWOT analysis of, 34–35
Technology inventory. *See also* Current technology environment, assessment of in technology plan
  data, 56
  hardware/operating system, 55
  network, 55
  network infrastructure, 54–55
  physical facilities, 54
  software, 55
  staff skills, 56–57
  technical support, 56
Technology plan
  incorporated in library's strategic plan, 2
  as part of larger organization's plan, 2
  need for, 1–2
  purposes of, 1–2, 3–7
  rationale for, 3–7
  separate, 2
  structure of
    assessment of current environment, 10
    challenges facing library, 9, 25–39
    current technology environment, 9
    description of library, 9, 13–23
    emerging technologies, 9
    evaluation of library's Web site, 9
    executive summary, 9
    plan for action, 10
    recommendations, 10
    updating, 10
  weaknesses of, 5
Technology planning, defined, 1
Technology planning committee
  role in planning, 7
Technology planning process
  model of, 6(fig.)
  parties involved in, 1–2, 7–8
  resources for, 8
Technology skill level chart (sample), 63(fig.)

Technology Trends for Libraries, 12
Telephony, 43
TEMPLES. *See under* SWOT
 analysis
Testing of Web services, 51
Texas Center for Educational
 Technology, 12
Transactions on Web Services, 50
Translation capabilities, 47
Transmission Control
 Protocol/Internet Protocol
 (TCP/IP), 42–43, 67, 78, 81
 and VOIP, 47

Ubiquity of Web services, 50
University of Michigan
 *President's Information
 Revolution Commission
 Report,* 3
University of Nevada at Las Vegas
 Library, 51
Updating technology plan
 defined, 10
 methods for assessing, 113–14
 need for, 111
 parties involved in, 114
 sample executive summary,
  115–17
 sample implementation plan
  tracking chart, 112

Vincent, Ida, 1
Virus protection, 56, 58
Vision statement, 25–26
 sample, 34
Voice and translation capabilities, 47
Voice Over Internet Protocol
 (VOIP), 47, 67
VoiceXML, 47

VOIP. *See* Voice Over Internet
 Protocol

Wal-Mart, and operational
 excellence, 32
Web Accessibility Initiative
 *Web Content Accessibility
 Guidelines* 1.0, 90
Web resources for planning, 10–12
Web services
 custom integration, 48
 middleware product, 38
 services, 48
  advantages of, 49–50
  problems with, 50–51
Web site design
 evaluation factors, 88–90
 features of, 85–86
 good, characteristics of, 86–87
 purpose/rationale for Web site, 85
 stages of Web site "life", 84–85
 usability guidelines, 88
Web sites
 evaluation of, defined, 10
Wide area network (WAN), 74
Wilson, William James, 99
Wireless connections, 46–47
Wireless fidelity (Wi-Fi), 46
World Wide Web Consortium
 (W3C), 47, 95
 Web Accessibility Initiative, *Web
  Content Accessibility
  Guidelines* 1.0, 90

XML. *See* Extensible Markup
 Language
XML MARC, 46
XML Schema Definition (XSD), 45

Z39.50 standard, 78

About the Author

JOSEPH R. MATTHEWS, internationally renowned expert on library automation and information systems, is president of his consulting company Matthews & Associates in Carlsbad, California.